"It is extremely important that we a_____ _____ _____ each other's spiritual practices and traditions, because to do so increases our opportunities for mutual respect. Sometimes, too, we encounter something in another tradition that helps us better appreciate something in our own. In *Mansions of the Spirit* Bishop Ingham draws on his own broad experience to take this inter-faith movement forward, exploring the place of Christianity among world religions"

— *His Holiness the Dalai Lama.*

"Bishop Michael Ingham gives an important stimulus for inter-faith dialogue and shows a hopeful way to the future: fidelity to Christianity and openness, mutual respect, and tolerance of other religions"

— *Hans Küng, University of Tübingen.*

"*Mansions of the Spirit* is magnificent. Probably I think that because I agree with it so completely. This book gives me hope that it's possible to save the tottering church, which I so dearly love, by listening, understanding as best we can, and knowing, without fear or hate, that God is Lord of all Creation, not just a special few among a special few. This is an important, indeed, essential book, written with both passion and compassion"

— *Madeleine L'Engle.*

"This is a book of engaging clarity on a subject of the greatest importance for biblical scholarship and, indeed, the intellectual honesty of all Christians"

— *The Rt. Revd Lord Runcie, former Archbishop of Canterbury.*

"Michael Ingham has written a closely argued and highly readable book that is essentially a deconstruction of Christian exclusivism. Of course, traditional Christianity is not the only religion claiming that it alone represents the true way to God, and therefore *Mansions of the Spirit* makes an important contribution to inter-religious rap-prochement. Given the often bloody history of religious strife, we badly need this affirmation of the old Jewish adage, 'The righteous of all nations have a share in salvation.'"

— *Rabbi W. Gunther Plaut.*

"Here is an important book that promises to help Christian people reach a greater understanding of their own faith in relation to other faiths. It should contribute greatly to mutual acceptance and constructive dialogue. It should also serve as an excellent introductory resource for seminary students and parish leaders searching for new ways to realize their vocation in a pluralistic world"
— *Abrahim H. Khan, Trinity College.*

"One of my consistent concerns as an inter-faith activist over the last fifteen or more years has been that our intellectual musings and interactions don't seem to be getting to the level of the pew. So Bishop Michael Ingham's *Mansions of the Spirit* comes as rain for a thirsty crop. Now we have a shepherd speaking to the flock directly and based in experience, hence from the heart. Written in simple straight-forward language, this succinct work is a persuasive argument for religious pluralism. I welcome it as a rare addition"
— *Suwanda H. J. Sugunasiri, Trinity College, Toronto.*

"Michael Ingham presents the issues at stake in a clear and simple manner. His survey of the history of inter-faith dialogue reveals how and why we have arrived where we currently are. This book will be extremely helpful and accessible to those taking their first steps in the field of inter-faith dialogue"
— *The Rev. Karen Hamilton, Inter-Church Inter-Faith Committee, United Church of Canada.*

Mansions of the Spirit

The Gospel in a Multi-Faith World

Michael Ingham

Anglican Book Centre
Toronto, Canada

1997
Anglican Book Centre
600 Jarvis Street
Toronto, Ontario
M4Y 2J6

Canadian Cataloguing in Publication Data

Ingham, Michael
    Mansions of the Spirit: The Gospel in a Multi-Faith World

ISBN 1-55126-185-5

1. Christianity and other religions. I. Title.

BR127.I53 1997   261.2   C97-930993-X

For Cara-Jayne and Robyn Joanna

with the prayer that they may one day
live in a world of religious peace

There will be no world peace without peace between the world's religions: there will be no peace between the world's religions without dialogue between the world's religions. —*Hans Küng*

I like diversity. I should no more want a world with one religion than I should want only one coloured rose in my garden. —*Rabbi Israel Mattuck*

Like the bee gathering honey from different flowers, the wise person sees only the good in all religions. —*Srimad Bhagavatam*

Nearest in love to the believers you will find those who say "We are Christians," because among them are those devoted to learning and those who have renounced the world, and they are not arrogant. —*The Koran*

Contents

Chapter One

An Unexpected Conversion

several years ago, I led a group of university students on a working visit to India. We were sponsored by the English Speaking Union, a group of internationally minded folk who believed strongly in the value of the British Commonwealth and sought to strengthen it by promoting contacts between people in the English-speaking world.

Most of us who visit other parts of the world, particularly the developing countries, have limited contact with local people. They serve us in hotels, or try to sell us things in the street. We stroll through their colourful markets and learn a bit of the fine art of haggling over prices. We watch dancers perform for us or buy attractive books to take home for the coffee table, and leave usually with a sense of having been stimulated by a way of life quite foreign to us, grateful for a taste of the exotic to take back to our very unexotic daily lives.

But few of us ever connect with the real lives of the people we meet in these situations. We hardly ever go into their homes or into the back rooms of their workplaces, or speak with them as we would with our neighbours at home. We learn little from these visits about the hardships of daily life, the struggles and joys, the hopes and fears of ordinary families leading ordinary lives. Still less do we get the opportunity to discuss religious beliefs or to learn about the spiritual practices that infuse the consciousness of the culture and shape the way life itself is experienced and lived by its people. All too often the impression Western tourists gain of other societies is glimpsed through the shaded windows of an air-conditioned bus.

Our visit to India was different. We were billeted separately in local homes in Bombay and put to work in schools or community organizations. I found myself in a household of twenty-six persons, organized along the lines of the traditional extended family, and spent my mornings trying (unsuccessfully) to be of some use in the Bombay Downtown YMCA. My hosts were Hindus, and I received from them the kind of hospitality one dreams of receiving when one is far from home. Many times since then, and in many other places, I have come to learn how hospitality is an art and a tradition in cultures outside the West, a deeply important obligation offered with grace and generosity and sometimes an almost ritual etiquette that contrasts starkly with our often relaxed informality and frequent indifference to the foreigner.

My Hindu hosts treated me with respect and curiosity. And when they learned of my faith as a Christian they were genuinely excited. They asked me to explain Christianity to them. They were interested to know more about Jesus, who he was, why I believed in him, whether I was in communication with him, and what messages I received. Night after night we talked about my religious beliefs. Their questions were intelligent and perceptive, although clearly framed from within their own thought forms and worldview, and sometimes so baffling that I often didn't know how to respond. But I was excited at this development and quickly came to the conclusion that God had sent me to this home in order to disclose the gospel and bring this family into the Christian fold. I was an enthusiastic young man in those days and didn't know, as I do now, that God had sent me there for entirely the opposite purpose.

One night, as I was in the full flood of explanation about some matter or other, the conversation took a sudden and unexpected turn. My hostess pronounced herself satisfied with what she had learned, and asked if I were interested in understanding their beliefs, their family rituals, and spiritual life—which I had observed from day to day, since the house held several small shrines decorated with colourful flowers, and I had been mystified by daily customs that clearly had a religious origin. She expected me to be as curious about their traditions as they had been about mine. Could she explain to me, and perhaps introduce me to, some of her own spiritual experiences and knowledge? Would I like to meet some important spiritual teachers in the city? They were as keen to share their experience of truth with me as I had been with them.

I was taken aback by the request. My first thought was that I had not sufficiently explained the Christian faith. I began to search for a way of re-doubling my persuasiveness, of convincing them conclusively about the uniqueness and finality of Jesus Christ, which had done away with other forms of worship and belief. But when I mentioned something to that effect, they lightly brushed it aside and told me that truth cannot be confined to any single path and that God's beauty and glory is demonstrated in many incarnations beyond the one called Jesus.

They took a hospitable pity on my limited spiritual understanding and, over the next few weeks, I was introduced to a variety of strange religious experiences. I had unexpectedly stimulating conversations with rather shabbily dressed gurus; I participated in seances, prayer meetings, and unusual forms of religious worship in which "messages" were transmitted from the spiritual world. Throughout these events, I armed myself with strong intellectual resistance, assuming the role of the sceptical observer, and, in the debriefing afterwards, always contested the interpretation placed upon the phenomena I had witnessed.

I think my hosts enjoyed these discussions as much as I did, but they never tried to convert me from Christianity. It was never their goal to lead me away from the path on which my soul was set. They simply wanted to broaden my horizons, to show me a bigger spiritual picture, and to offer me their love, which genuinely grew between us as the time passed. My hostess believed strongly that the root of all

human unhappiness is false desire. We create our own dis-
appointments by seeking for ourselves what God has not intended.
"Desire nothing for yourself," she would say, "and all joy will come
to you." I later discovered that this was one of the teachings of the
Buddha, but there are many echoes of it in the words of Jesus.

From that day to this, I have never been tempted to become a
Hindu or to seek a deeper communion with God through anyone
other than Christ. It is enough for me to try to become a better
Christian, to open myself more and more to God's grace in Christ;
and that will be a lifelong task in itself. Unlike many of my friends in
earlier days, I was never drawn to experimenting with different
religious traditions, hopping about from one faith to another in
spiritual disorientation, or borrowing bits of one religion and sticking
it together with bits of another to create something I could wholly
believe. I am, for better or worse, a disciple of Christ, or I try to be,
and with all its difficulties, his is the only path for me.

But I was deeply impressed by that most attractive of Hinduism's
characteristics—the willingness to look for the divine in many different
guises, the confidence that God can be known, worshipped, and
adored in a multiplicity of ways, the non-absoluteness of Hindu
claims to knowledge of ultimate truth without any lessening of
personal discipline or effort at serving it.

In the years that have followed my visit to India, I have often
asked myself why this has never been part of my experience of
Christianity. What is it that makes Christians so assured of the
rightness of our understanding of God that we are unable to think we
might have something to learn from the Jew, the Muslim, the
Buddhist? What is it, in our faith and the faith of others, that leads to
religious bigotry and intolerance? I have frequently been saddened
by the attitudes of colleagues and friends in my own church whose
certitude about their theological position contrasts so starkly with the
spiritual humility and openness of many in other religious traditions
whose depth of intimacy with God is evident and radiant.

Today I have come to believe it is possible, and increasingly
necessary, to look into our own religious tradition and ask ourselves
whether such attitudes are an essential part of the Christian gospel. I
see a number of reasons for this. There is a growing inter-faith
movement throughout the world that can no longer be regarded as a
fringe development at the edges of the world's religions. There is a

deep desire for dialogue and mutual understanding among many adherents of different religious traditions. Within the church there is less certainty today among biblical scholars about the historical foundation of the sayings attributed to Jesus upon which Christian triumphalism and absolutism have been based. There are reasons to doubt the wisdom and truth of doctrines that justify claims to religious superiority. And there is the sheer fact of the massive global relocation of religious populations, which has brought us face to face with people of other traditions.

Perhaps the place to begin, therefore, is with ourselves, with what is happening in our own neighbourhoods and communities.

Chaper 2

Who Is My Neighbour?

*I*n this century we have seen the phenomenon of the global migration of peoples on a scale never before witnessed in our history—not only vast movements of refugees within continents like Europe and Africa, but the resettlement of migrant workers and immigrants far from their countries of origin in almost all parts of the world. In North America, as elsewhere, we now live and work alongside people of different ethnic and racial groups, and for the first time we are coming into contact with the religions of the world embodied in human faces and next-door-neighbour families. The relationship, therefore, between Christianity and the world's religions is no longer an academic question.

This is a new phenomenon. Before the twentieth century, most of the great religions of the world were separated from one another geographically. The religions of Europe, Asia, and Africa, for example, had little contact with each other in the course of day to day commerce. They usually met only on the battlefield.

Christians and Muslims, for instance, have tended to encounter each other principally in territorial warfare. The emergence of Islam in Arabia in the sixth century was followed by its rapid spread into North Africa—then the seat and stronghold of Christianity after the collapse of the Roman Empire in Europe. Here the ground was laid for centuries of competition and conflict. Islam won over many African converts from Christianity and gradually Islamicized the region south of the Mediterranean Sea. The Muslim conquest of Spain in the eighth century represented a threat to Europe itself in the eyes of the church, and was eventually repulsed by Christian armies after hundreds of years of fighting. The Crusades from the eleventh to the fourteenth centuries were an effort to take back the territory of the Holy Land from Islamic control and to expand Western power eastwards. This history of hostility has laid deep roots of suspicion between Christians and Muslims, which shapes mutual attitudes today.

Similar histories have disfigured the relationships between other global religions too. Buddhism began in India in the sixtth century B.C.E. and grew up within the fold of Hinduism, but Buddhism challenged the orthodoxy of Hinduism's beliefs, especially its sacrificial system, and opposed the stratified social structure that separated people into castes. While traditional Hindu accommodation of diversity allowed co-existence with Buddhism to continue for over a thousand years, tensions were often high and Buddhism found more receptive audiences for its missionary efforts outside India. It was largely driven out of the sub-continent by Turkish Muslims in the twelfth century.

Christians and Jews have similarly had a tragic history of bitterness. The origins of the Christian community were of course within the Jewish religion. The first Christians regarded themselves— and were regarded by the religious authorities of Israel—as a sect within Judaism. Indeed, the New Testament proclaims Christ as the fulfilment of Jewish messianic expectation, and its earliest books presuppose the disciples' membership in the synagogue.

As the missionary work of the apostles spread outside the Jewish community into the Greco-Roman world, however, tensions arose within the apostolic community as to what disciplines and rules were to be required of the Gentile converts. The circumcision controversy reported in Paul's letters and the Book of Acts, and the disputes around the preparation of food and the eating of sacrifices offered to idols, were precisely about how Jewish the new Christian sect was to remain. Claiming the authority of the Holy Spirit, the early church chose to proclaim Christ as liberator from the Jewish law. A new covenant was proclaimed in place of the old. The church announced salvation through Christ alone. Not surprisingly, the emergence of Christianity as an alternative to Judaism produced a reaction within the parent body, and resulted in hostility and the persecution of Christian heretics by some local leaders of synagogues.

Herein lie the seeds of anti-Semitism within Christianity. We shall look later at some of the anti-Jewish texts in the gospels, and consider whether they did in fact come from the lips of Jesus or whether they may reflect later circumstances in the church at the time the gospels came to be written down. This is a hotly disputed issue among modern biblical scholars. But what is not deniable is the history of Christian-Jewish relationships that followed in Europe and its tragic consequences for Jewry—involving centuries of slander, hatred, violence, legalized denial of rights, pogroms, and slaughter— culminating this century in the organized murder of six million Jews within a supposedly Christian nation.

One can document endlessly the stories of religious warfare and savagery that have bedeviled human societies from the dawn of time. They arise both between religions and within each of them. Their consequences have been momentous in shaping the world in which we live today.

But our modern context is significantly different from the past. The religious philosopher John Hick has pointed out that historically the religions of the world have been coterminous with the cultures of the world. Each society has expressed its own cultural life through a distinctive religious tradition. And before now, the world's societies have been geographically separated—most religious conflicts have taken place between contiguous or adjacent cultural and religious groups. But today the world's peoples are interconnected culturally and economically, and more and more our modern post-industrial societies are becoming multi-cultural and multi-ethnic as the peoples of the world come to live side by side with each other. As the title of a recent report on multi-culturalism by the Anglican Church of Canada stated it, we are *No Longer Strangers*. This presents new challenges but also new opportunities for mutual understanding among peoples of differing religions.

Our situation today is perceptively expressed in a paper prepared by the Church of England in 1988 and presented to the Lambeth Conference of Anglican bishops:

> Within living memory every religion tended to be restricted to specific parts of the world. If one wished to see Buddhism at first-hand it was necessary to travel to Ceylon or Japan. Now the Chiswick Vihara has some twenty thousand people on its mailing list, and saffron-robed monks walk the Sussex lanes or the streets of Wolverhampton. A Japanese peace pagoda rises on a lakeside in Milton Keynes and another is to tower above the western suburbs of London.
>
> Muslims lived, then, in Arabia overspilling into North Africa, and eastward into Persia and India. (Even then our ideas were restricted, few of us realizing that Indonesia was to become the largest Muslim nation.) Now among Nash's terraces surrounding Regent's Park the great dome of a splendid mosque symbolizes the presence of nearly a million Muslims in the United Kingdom—most of whom are not exotic visitors from oil rich states but fellow-citizens with us. They make vital contributions to Britain's economic well-being and social life. So even Church Schools in some Northern and Midland cities now may be almost entirely composed of Muslim pupils.
>
> Hindus were properly the citizens of the Indian Empire (indeed, their name signifies not so much their religious beliefs as the land to which they belonged). Now Leicester has the largest Hindu community, after Durban, outside India; and Birmingham and Wolverhampton, Manchester and Leeds, Coventry and Bristol, as well as dozens of much smaller towns, have flourishing temples and celebrate Hindu festivals like *diwali*.
>
> Sikhs, too, have left their ancestral homes in north-west India, or have been expelled by various regimes from their adopted countries in East Africa. Some two hundred thousand of these "disciples" (for this is what the word "Sikh" means)

are now settled in Britain: the Woolwich *gurdwara* (just one example) counts its adherents as fifteen thousand.

Nor should we forget the Chinese "diaspora" scattered the length and breadth of these islands. New research is discovering how much of the old religions of China is still being practised among them. There are, too, smaller communities of Jains, of Zoroastrians, and of Baha'is, many of these last refugees from the appalling persecutions taking place in modern Iran.

So the religious map is altered, in the world and in our own country. We need only note here that our British experience is paralleled in every Western European country; nearly six million Muslims live in Common Market countries. It is matched too in Canada and in South Africa; both Toronto and Durban claim to be the most multi-religious cities in the world, and of course in the USA.

In Britain, as in many other countries, Christians, Muslims, Hindus and people of other faiths work together in the same shops, offices and factories, study together in the same schools and colleges, travel on the same buses and trains, work together in the same hospitals and public services, pay the same taxes and are represented by the same Members of Parliament.

Many people find this religious and cultural mixture a novel and bewildering experience. Not only Christians, but people of other faiths as well, find it strange to work as colleagues or be neighbours with people who hold different beliefs and observe different customs, who keep different religious festivals and holidays, and who profess allegiance to different religious teachers. Sometimes Christians admire the devotion and loyalty to their faith of those of other religions. They are challenged by the deep springs of faith, wisdom and spirituality, the willingness to accept the demanding rules and discipline of their faith and the close fellowship and commitment to the family, often the extended family, that characterises the lives of others.

In all this they challenge Christians to rethink their own beliefs and practices. More often, however, differences and strangeness divides and alienates the different religious communities. Genuine fear of that which is strange develops, sometimes leading to extreme behaviour as one community seeks to exclude and hurt that which it does not understand and which it can only perceive in terms of a threat. Rivalries and jealousies between groups lead to violence which destroys any possibility of living with creative diversity (*Towards A Theology for Inter-Faith Dialogue;* Lambeth Conference Paper, 1988).

Western urban society is now culturally and religiously pluralistic in ways that urgently raise the biblical question, "Who is my neighbour?" In the Christian tradition, love of neighbour has been an ethical imperative from the beginning, coming directly from the lips of Jesus: "Love the Lord your God with all your heart, with all your soul, with all your mind, and with all your strength; and love your neighbour as yourself" (Matt. 22:9). The teaching is not an isolated text, but is repeated in all the synoptic gospels in a variety of ways (Matt. 19:9; Mark 12:31; Luke 10:27). The Letter of James calls it the "royal law" (James 2:8). Paul describes it as the summation of the law (Rom. 13:9).

This teaching is not original to Jesus. The obligation to love one's neighbour had long been part of the Jewish law (Lev. 19:18). So too was the command to love God (Deut. 6:5). Both were part of the Torah, the fundamental instruction of Hebrew Scripture. Jesus, however, linked them together. He made love of God and love of neighbour a corollary of each other, and this linkage was a unique aspect of his teaching. Jesus supported and strengthened the orthodox tenets of his own religious tradition in urging this ethic upon his disciples and the church.

In fact, it was the issue of neighbourliness that prompted perhaps the most famous of all the parables of Jesus, the story of the good Samaritan. In response to a question from a lawyer (Luke 10:25) who wanted a definition of neighbour, Jesus gave the powerful illustration that has come down through the centuries as one of the central principles of Christian faith.

The point of the parable is not simply the importance of compassion for the less fortunate. Jesus was not merely saying, "Give somebody a helping hand." The point is that our neighbour is whoever God sets in our path, whomever we meet along our way. Our neighbour is not necessarily someone like us, our kin, someone we recognize from our own tribal, racial, or ideological group. Our neighbour may be an alien or even an enemy. It is whoever is in need, whoever is thrust upon us. Christians are obligated to care, not simply for our own, but for all whom God brings before us in our daily routines.

Christians therefore do not have a choice about this ethic, nor do we have a choice about our neighbours. The modern world has made neighbours of us all, whether we like it or not, and so the ethical imperative now has a global dimension that impinges upon us in very practical and local ways.

Inter-faith cooperation and dialogue must now be seen as one aspect of this imperative. It is not enough simply to acknowledge the pluralism of our societies as if we were noting a change in the weather. What we do now with respect to the growing convergence and interpenetration of religious communities will have profound consequences for the unfolding of our future.

The Dangers of Intolerance

Roman Catholic scholar Hans Küng, in a much quoted comment, has said, "There will be no world peace without peace between the world's religions: there will be no peace between the world's religions without dialogue between the world's religions" (*Global Responsibility: In Search of a New World Ethic*, 1991). The truth of this warning seems axiomatic. Dialogue and mutual understanding is a much better avenue towards our global future than violence and war. Within our own lifetimes we have witnessed the failures of religious leaders and religious peoples to build bridges of tolerance and respect in polarized and dangerous circumstances. Bosnia, Lebanon, Israel, Sudan, Nigeria, Sri Lanka, Kashmir, Punjab, and Northern Ireland are all examples of conflict across religious lines that have claimed hundreds of thousands of lives just within the last twenty years.

Violence on this scale is never simply a result of religious disagreements, of course. There are always political, economic, and social causes at the root of the problem. They all get mixed up together, and sometimes the religious labels are simply convenient ways of identifying the separate parties. "Protestant extremists" and

"Catholic extremists" are names given by the media to the terrorists in Northern Ireland, though neither group has any spiritual connection with Christianity. The gunmen of both camps ignore the pleas of responsible and representative Irish church leaders, as well as the fervent prayers of people around the world.

The fact is that religious and ethnic identity often go together, and when ethnic conflict arises, it inevitably takes on a religious dimension. When different groups of people belong to the same culture but come from different racial or socio-economic backgrounds, the defining difference between them is often the religion they follow. So Protestants and Catholics are divided in Northern Ireland not because there is anything in Protestantism or Catholicism that compels them to be divided, but because these labels are used to distinguish communities from each other and give each one their separate identity.

Orthodox versus Catholic. Catholic versus Protestant. Christian versus Muslim or Jew. How can anyone be expected to believe in the God all these people worship? How could anyone find attractive or credible a religion that supports such inhuman cruelty? How could any tradition condone the merciless barbarity in the name of God that we see nightly on our television screens?

The answer, of course, is that God doesn't. No authentic religious tradition of any stripe endorses ethnic butchery. The Serbian Orthodox church, the Catholic church in Croatia, and the Islamic authorities in Bosnia all condemned the atrocities there. The Canadian Council of Churches, the Conference of European Churches, the World Council of Churches, and others around the world called for a negotiated peace in the Balkans and an end to the violence. No religious body sanctions what we are seeing today. But the gunmen who shoot at defenceless schoolchildren and rape innocent women are far from the reach of religious leaders. They are consumed with a malevolent hatred that makes them deaf to the call for compassion and the respect for human rights that is being urged by faith communities of every sort.

These tragedies create such lasting and permanent bitterness in the minds of their victims that they write the memories into their history, even their sacred history and their sacred texts. Conflict becomes part of the historic consciousness, the identity, of a people in such a way that it creates and recreates new violence in each succeeding generation. Ancient and savage memories run deep, scores are settled and resettled for years afterwards, until hatred becomes a permanent condition of human relationships and reconciliation is all but impossible.

But while religious faith cannot be deemed the sole cause of these brutalities, and the complexity of ethnic conflict must not be oversimplified, nevertheless no faith tradition can escape responsibility for the consequences of religious destructiveness. Every world religion has had a social, political, and environmental impact on the current human condition and must be viewed objectively and critically from a moral perspective. John Hick writes,

> Hinduism, though constituting an immensely rich and powerful universe of meaning ... also validates the hierarchical caste system of India including the relegation of millions to the position of outcasts ... and still tolerates the cruel persecution and sometimes murder of brides whose dowry is deemed insufficient.

> Buddhism, although basically peaceful and tolerant ... has been indifferent until very recently to questions of social justice, so that many Buddhist lands have long remained in a state of feudal inequality.

> Islam ... though notably free from colour prejudice, has sanctioned "holy wars," fanatical intolerance, and the barbaric punishments of mutilation and flogging, and still generally consigns women to a protected but narrowly confined life.

> Christianity, though providing a birthplace for modern science and a home for modern liberal ideas of equality and freedom, has generated savage wars of religion and supported innumerable "just wars"; has tortured and burned multitudes of heretics and witches in the name of God; has motivated and authorized the persecution of Jews; has validated systematic racism; and has tolerated the Western capitalist "rape of the earth," the misuse of nuclear energy, and the basic injustice of the North-South division into rich and poor nations (*The Non-Absoluteness of Christianity*, 1987).

We will have to come to terms with our own history as Christians if we wish to avoid the dangers of renewed and sustained religious intolerance in our increasingly pluralistic society. For pluralism by itself does not ensure tolerance or peaceful co-existence. There will have to be a willingness to confront honestly the failures of our tradition, as well as its glories and achievements, if we are to have any hope of being credible participants in a dialogue with people of other religions and of creating a new future together.

As Archbishop Desmond Tutu wrote before the end of apartheid in South Africa in 1991, "Repentance and forgiveness are indispensable for setting right relationships between those who have been wronged and wrongdoers within nations and between nations. Unless you deal with the past in a creative and positive manner then you run the terrible risk of having no future worth speaking about" (*Anglican Communion News Service*).

Every participant in inter-faith dialogue, therefore, should require of himself or herself an attitude of penitence and humility with respect to the tradition they represent. From a strictly moral perspective, no tradition has a valid claim to triumphalism or self-righteousness. "All have sinned. All have fallen short of the glory of God" (Rom. 3:23). The goal of inter-faith dialogue is not to point out the faults of the other community, but discussion cannot proceed without mutual acknowledgment of the suffering that has been inflicted on one another, and by accepting appropriate responsibility for the mistakes of the past. As the former World Religions Sub-Committee of the Anglican Church of Canada puts it,

> With our new neighbours of different traditions, we do not simply displace all that they hold dear with some European brand of Christianity. Rather we enter into dialogue with them, expecting to say "yes" and "no" to their history, as we say "yes" and "no" to our own, and prepared to hear their "yes" and "no" to our culture from the perspective of their spiritual grounding (*An Anglican Basis for Inter-Faith Encounters*, 1986).

This dialectical, or "yes" and "no" approach, is an essential step in avoiding the defensiveness that frustrates honesty and defeats genuine progress in building up new kinds of community. We do not need to feel we must defend everything in the Christian tradition. And much can be accomplished, many doors opened, when our partners in dialogue learn this about us.

Religion as a Positive Spiritual Force

The impetus for inter-faith dialogue in our new context of pluralism is not simply a negative one. It's not just that societies can fall apart into internecine savagery if justice and tolerance are not carefully developed. There are positive reasons for people of all religions to adopt new attitudes of openness and accommodation towards each other. These have to do with harnessing the enormous power of religious traditions to deepen spiritual qualities of respect and trust, to unite the peoples of the world in common action, and to point us to the transcendent and ultimate reality of God which relativizes and judges all our human endeavours.

Religion can be a powerful force for good as well as for evil. The majority of the world's peoples are deeply religious, and the various spiritual traditions play an important role in providing the belief systems and worldview within which we act out our lives. In differing ways, all of them call for the highest ideals and the noblest truths to be sovereign in human affairs.

Every faith community has an ethical core which exerts a strong influence over the formation of individual conscience and personal behaviour. And religious faith globally is still the most successful countervailing influence to materialistic visions of progress, which appeal to self-interest and greed rather than love.

Despite all the horrors of history, we can see where faith has inspired people to heroic acts of self-sacrifice and courage in defence of justice and peace. In our own day, the role of the churches in South Africa in the peaceful dismantling of an oppressive system of racism is a good example. In that country, the church was the only organized body of opposition that was not successfully exiled or imprisoned by the apartheid regime. But there are other examples too.

The role of the church in East Germany and Poland was critical in undermining the foundations of Soviet Communism in eastern Europe. In the Middle East, Christians, Muslims, and Jews have acted together in solidarity for a negotiated settlement of the Israeli-Palestinian dispute. All over the world, in local industrial or social conflicts, respected religious leaders are involved in mediation and reconciliation work, offering the good offices of their faith traditions to cool down inflamed passions and to foster improved relationships.

One of the most significant appeals to the world's religions in recent times has come from members of the scientific community.

The 1993 Parliament of the World's Religions in Chicago began with a presentation by a group of international scientists about the crisis in the earth's biosphere. In a report entitled *Global 2000 Revisited,* they documented the pressures on global resources caused by population growth, the degradation of the ozone layer, the destruction of agricultural land, the pollution of the oceans and the atmosphere, and the rapid decline of the gene pool. At the conclusion, they said,

> Given the magnitude of the issues we face, we must expect that within the lifetime of a child born today, the world will change radically in one of two directions. If we continue with present beliefs, institutions, and policies, the world will become highly polarized, with a billion people in the wealthy industrialized countries of the North attempting to enjoy life and leisure a few decades longer while 10 billion plus people in the South spiral downward into increasingly desperate poverty exacerbated by global environmental deterioration (*Global 2000 Revisited,* 1993).

They called this the dawn of a new dark age. But what the scientists said last of all was critical. They said the fundamental crisis in our world is not environmental, or economic, or political. The fundamental crisis is spiritual. It has to do with attitudes, beliefs, and practices. It has to do with the way we live and the way we relate to other life on the planet, both human and animal. The crisis will not be solved by science or technology, nor by politicians.

The solution, they said, lies in the rediscovery of spiritual values that empower people to change and lead new lives. They quoted former UN Secretary-General Dag Hammarskjöld, an economist, who said, "Unless the world has a spiritual rebirth, civilisation is doomed." And in a letter to the spiritual leaders of the world they wrote,

> We, the people of Earth, need the help and involvement of our spiritual leaders. It is from our respective faiths that we derive our sense of origins, of self, of purpose, of possibility. You are our source of inspiration for what we humans and Earth can become. Your dreams are our visions—and our destiny. We depend on you (Gerald O. Barney, *A Letter to Our Spiritual Leaders,* 1993).

An appeal like this illustrates both the hope that is still invested in the world's spiritual movements to bring about a new world order, and the responsibility of these movements to use their faith as a positive force for global harmony and environmental responsibility.

Paradoxically, it is the inertia that is often demonstrated by traditional religions with respect to the environmental crisis that is giving rise to new spiritual movements outside the historic traditions. In the Western world, the fastest growing new religious movements are those focusing on environmental spirituality, eco-feminism, and the recovery of Aboriginal spirituality. Though the historic religions are rich in resources for addressing the pressing environmental crisis, their failure to do so is turning globally conscious people towards various forms of pantheism and paganism in order to find spiritual grounding for their lives.

Yet even this illustrates the point. The recovery of a spiritual vision and ethical practice must be the basis of action and hope for the world. Political and scientific solutions can only be achieved if there is a conversion of mind and spirit among the world's peoples on a vast scale. Robert Müller, a career diplomat and former Assistant Secretary-General of the United Nations, writes,

> Religions and spiritual traditions: the world needs you very much! You, more than anyone else, have experience, wisdom, insights and feeling for the miracle of life, of the Earth and of the universe. After having been pushed aside in many fields of human endeavour, you must again be the lighthouse, the guides, the prophets and messengers of the ultimate mysteries of the universe and eternity. You must set up the mechanisms to agree, and you must give humanity the divine or cosmic rules for our behaviour on this planet (*A Source Book for the Community of Religions*, 1993).

The inter-faith movement, as well as the world's religious traditions individually, has an important contribution to make to the evolution of this desperately needed sense of global responsibility.

Chapter Three

The Inter-Faith Movement

The term *movement* is misleading when applied to the many people and organizations involved in inter-faith dialogue. It suggests a single entity with a formal structure. In fact, the inter-faith movement is not a structure so much as an organism, a dynamic and multiplying organism made up of many cells. Or to change the analogy, it is not so much a river as a collection of many streams, each springing from different origins and flowing sometimes together and sometimes separately towards the same ocean.

Let me summarize very briefly some of the main streams of the inter-faith movement to illustrate the wide variety of interest and concerns that have compelled people all over the world to work together across religious boundaries.

1893 Parliament of the World's Religions

A desire for convergence among the great religious traditions of the world began to emerge among significant numbers of people towards the end of the nineteenth century. This period, we may recall, was one of extraordinary creativity and change, especially in the Western world. Charles Darwin had begun to challenge accepted religious and scientific theories about the natural order. The Industrial Revolution was changing the face of nations and creating new urban communities. Colonial expansion had created an explosion of international trade. There was a growing cross-fertilization of cultural and spiritual ideas, particularly among educated elites.

It was a time when many Western intellectuals had begun to develop scientific ideas about evolution into a general theory of cultural and spiritual progress. Technological advances, new access to remote and distant cultures, and a deepening secularism in the West that challenged traditional religious beliefs, all encouraged a growing openness to new ideas and stimulated speculation about the inexorable progress of human civilization towards higher and higher levels of social and spiritual development.

The New World idealism of the emerging United States was also beginning to exert a global influence. And it was in America that the modern inter-faith movement was born.

In 1893, the city of Chicago hosted the World Exposition. It was intended to be a showcase of American technology and political optimism. In connection with it, a group of visionary individuals decided to mount the first organized gathering of representatives from the major world religions. This gathering, the first Parliament of the World's Religions, marks the beginning of the modern inter-faith movement, which is now just over a hundred years old. It brought together about four hundred official delegates, mostly Americans and mostly males but with guests from around the world, and was the occasion for the first major cooperative effort among American Jews, Catholics, and Protestants.

The ideals of the parliament were expressed in some of its preliminary propositions:

a) There is a coming unity of mankind in the service of God and man.

b) There is an influx from God into the mind of every man, teaching that there is a God and that he should be worshipped and obeyed; and that as the light of the sun is differently received by different objects, so the light of divine revelation is differently received by different minds, and hence arise varieties in the forms of religion.

c) Those who believe in these things may work together for the welfare of mankind, notwithstanding, they may differ in the opinions they hold respecting God, His revelation and manifestation, and that such fraternity does not require the surrender of the points of difference (Marcus Braybrooke, *Pilgrimage of Hope*, 1992).

These propositions express some of the enduring principles of the inter-faith movement. Its fundamental vision is that of human unity, the desire among many religious adherents to build a new global community through spiritual means. It has a simple theoretical or doctrinal foundation that envisages the different religions of the world as simply different expressions of belief in the same God. And it celebrates the differences among religions, holding these differences to be of positive value, rather than attempting to harmonize them into a single belief system that negates the uniqueness of each tradition.

It is a vision best captured in images rather than concepts. The light of the sun, reflecting marvellously and in different ways throughout the earth, is an image expressive of the one God—the light of the world—who is worshipped by people of different cultures in distinctive, but not mutually negating, ways. Other images depict rivers flowing into a single ocean, or separate pearls held together on a single string. These are ventures into poetry rather than theology. They are creative leaps of the religious imagination reaching towards an unformulated, but deeply felt, theological consensus among a growing number of the world's faithful.

The parliament was dominated by Christian delegates, and it is clear from many of the speeches that most of them believed Christianity to be the highest form of revelation from God, and that it was the destiny of other religions to be subsumed eventually into the Christian fold. Following Darwin's evolutionary theory, they believed that the lower must give way to the higher in the spiritual progress of humankind. One who challenged this assumption, however, and made a great impact on the conference, was the Hindu leader Swami Vivekananda.

Vivekananda was from Calcutta and a disciple of the great Hindu teacher Ramakrishna. He was an articulate and powerful speaker and, during the course of the conference, emerged as one of its most popular figures, particularly among the American press. Vivekananda impressed his hearers with dynamic presentations of the Hindu vision of the many-sidedness of truth, allowing for a variety of spiritual paths, each streaming towards the same goal. Some of his comments, delivered over the course of the event, give a flavour of his appeal:

> Do not care for doctrines, do not care for dogmas or sects or churches or temples; they count for little compared with the essence of existence in each man which is spirituality.

> All religions, from the lowest fetishism to the highest absolutism, are so many attempts of the human soul to grasp and realize the Infinite, as determined by the condition of birth and association.

> The varieties of religion are adapted to the varieties of the human personality and development.

> In the Bhagavad Gita, the Lord Krishna says: "I am in every religion as the thread through a string of pearls."

> Every religion is only an evolving of God out of material man. The same God is the inspirer of all.

> I am proud to belong to a religion which has taught the world both tolerance and universal acceptance. We believe not only in universal toleration, but we accept all religions as true (*Pilgrimage of Hope*, 1992).

Vivekananda's typical Hindu pluralism appealed to the late nineteenth century's emerging ideals of universalism and global progress. It was the first time many Americans had heard such a clear and compelling vision of universal tolerance and spiritual harmony. And it contrasted with the position commonly associated with the church. For not all Christians shared in the Swami's spiritual generosity, nor in the liberal optimism of the day.

One of those who opposed the 1893 parliament, and declined an invitation to attend, was the Archbishop of Canterbury, Dr. Benson. In a letter to the assembly stating his objection to its very concept, he wrote, "The Christian religion is the one religion. I do not understand how that one religion can be regarded as a member of a Parliament of

Religions, without assuming the equality of other intended members and the parity of their position and claims" (*Pilgrimage of Hope*, 1992).

Clearly, the vision of Vivekananda was not warmly welcomed everywhere. The archbishop's position was reflected in a resolution affirmed four years later by the Lambeth Conference of Anglican bishops: "That the tendency of many English-speaking Christians to entertain an exaggerated opinion of the excellences of Hinduism and Buddhism, and to ignore the fact that Jesus Christ alone has been constituted Saviour and King of mankind, should be vigorously corrected" (*Lambeth Conference*, 1897; Resolution 15).

This objection, characteristic of the theological school known as exclusivism (which we shall explore further in Chapter 4), represented the largely unquestioned assumptions of the church at that time. Yet even then it did not command universal acceptance. When Benson's letter was read to the assembly, an Anglican delegate responded with a speech critical of its churlish spirit. In the course of it, he made an interesting observation: "The fact is, all religions are fundamentally more or less true, and all religions are superficially more or less false."

This is an intriguing distinction and raises many further questions. What is the fundamental truth of all religions? Who can claim to know this, and upon what authority? On what grounds do we distinguish between the fundamental and the superficial elements in religion? Why should only the superficial ones be false? Is there a single religion underlying all the others?

Reactions such as those of the Anglican Communion at the time, and of other official religious institutions, illustrate some of the complex issues raised by the inter-faith movement. In a real sense, the last hundred years has produced a radical challenge to the traditional self-understanding of the world's religions, a challenge not from outside but from within the spiritual communities themselves, mounted by people seeking to broaden the central concepts of neighbour and of God.

We shall explore later some of the theological issues that are being addressed by proponents and opponents of inter-faith dialogue. But for now, let us follow the growth of the movement after its beginnings in Chicago.

The first Parliament of the World's Religions was a single event. It did not meet again until 1993 when it marked its own centenary. It left no continuing structure. Its purpose was simply to create new bonds of friendship and to act as a sign of spiritual cooperation. Other people sought to strengthen the inter-faith movement by establishing small but permanent organizations.

World Congress of Faiths

One of these is the World Congress of Faiths (WCF). The creation of a British army officer, Sir Francis Younghusband, the WCF dates back to 1934. Its purpose is to develop a "fellowship of faiths"—a community in which people may awaken to God through a wider consciousness of the Spirit—as distinct from a single world religion.

The first gathering of the congress was in London in 1936. This brought together outstanding academic scholars of different religious traditions—Muslim lawyers, Russian Orthodox Christians, Hindu philosophers, Chinese historians, Jewish leaders, Buddhist teachers, as well as Mormons, Jains, Baha'is, and humanists. The papers were of a high quality, though they revealed varying attitudes towards theological issues. Some felt that the goal of a single world religion was desirable and even achievable. Others stressed the necessary plurality of divine revelation among the different cultures of the world. A comment by Rabbi Dr. Israel Mattuck of the World Union for Progressive Judaism is particularly striking: "I like diversity. I should no more want a world with one religion than I should want only one coloured rose in my garden. We can have diversity without enmity, and when we do this, I believe, the world will be more ready to receive our message about human unity and human peace" (*World Congress of Faiths*, 1936).

Here we find echoes of the teaching of Jesus in John's gospel in which he prays for a communion of such depth and power among those who believe in him that the world may see and believe (John 17:23). The London conference thus articulated what people in the inter-faith movement have come to believe: that it is the scandal of enmity between God's people—not the fact of diversity—that prevents the growth of faith among millions of people, who are dissuaded from any religious path by our mutual anathemas.

The idea of fellowship among believers has been the dominant theme of the WCF. In the years since the first conference there have been many global assemblies, and a small continuing structure has been formed with an office in England.

Significantly, a recent meeting in 1986 featured a lecture by another Archbishop of Canterbury. Taking a very different position from that of his predecessor, Dr. Benson, in 1893, Archbishop Robert Runcie said,

> Dialogue can help us recognize that other faiths than our own are genuine mansions of the Spirit with many rooms to be discovered, rather than solitary fortresses to be attacked.
>
> Without losing our respective identities and the precious heritage and roots of our faith ... by relating our respective visions of the Divine to each other, we can discover a still greater splendour of divine life and grace.
>
> From the perspective of *faith,* different world religions can be seen as different gifts of the Spirit to humanity.
>
> I am not advocating a single minded and synthetic model of world religion. What I want is for each tradition, and especially my own, to break through its own particularity (*Pilgrimage of Hope,* 1992).

This shift in perspective among Anglican leaders is also reflected in the statements of the Lambeth Conference over the last one hundred years. From indignant condemnation of the "exaggerated opinion of the excellences of Hinduism and Buddhism," the bishops of the Anglican Communion in their most recent statements have moved to a deeper awareness of the richness of spiritual diversity among the world's peoples (see Appendix A).

In fact, although it is not my purpose here, an interesting study can be made of Lambeth Conference statements on this subject, for they reveal the kind of theological wrestling with the issues of our multi-religious world in a way that shows the classic Anglican instinct to remain faithful to Christian tradition while being open to the world. One can discern in them, even from a cursory glance at the range of statements on the subject since the first gathering in 1867, a definite movement away from exclusionary dismissal of the non-Christian world toward cautious desire for peaceful co-existence with the great religions of humankind. They do not go as far as many individual Anglicans would like, and much further than others wish to see, yet they exemplify the gradual shift in the inter-faith climate evident in global movements throughout this century.

The WCF, however, has been able to move much further in several areas than any of the mainstream Christian bodies. One significant development has been in inter-faith worship. A common practice at congress gatherings has been to include worship as a central element in the proceedings. Typically, this involves a selection of prayers and sacred readings drawn from the different traditions present. Leadership is offered by several participants, and music is chosen with care so that the words of hymns, for example, can be sung by everyone together.

The planning of these services takes great care, and has met some opposition from traditionalist quarters, but offers a useful model for inter-faith groups elsewhere whose level of trust is developing to the point where they can pray together.

International Association for Religious Freedom

Another stream of the global movement is the International Association for Religious Freedom (IARF). This is one of the oldest and most experienced inter-faith organizations worldwide. It owes its origins to the Unitarian church and dates back to 1900.

Unitarians, regarded as theologically suspect by Christian churches because of their rejection of the doctrines of the Trinity and the divinity of Christ, have long been at the forefront of social and ethical issues such as justice, peace, and liberty. Shaped historically by nineteenth-century liberal and rational traditions, they were early pioneers in the inter-faith movement.

IARF's founder was Charles Wendte, a German-American who was pastor of an inner-city church in Chicago that became famous for its relief work among the poor. In his memoirs, Wendte describes a moment in his church's soup kitchen when he watched a local rabbi carve slices of bacon from a pork roast being held by a Catholic priest as together they served a meal to the hungry. This experience convinced him that religious taboos could be overcome for the sake of the human family.

Wendte organized the first conference in Boston in 1900 (though its name at that time was the International Council of Unitarians and Other Liberal Religious Thinkers). Other conferences followed, and the tireless work of Charles Wendte gradually built up an international organization that attracted liberal Christians, Jews, Muslims, and members of the Brahmo Samaj, a Hindu Reform movement. At the Berlin Conference of 1910, over two thousand people attended, among them the leading German liberal theologians Ernst Troeltsch (whom we shall meet in Chapter 6) and Adolf von Harnack.

Today the IARF concentrates its work on securing freedom of religious belief and worship in the member states of the United Nations. It intervenes on behalf of prisoners of conscience and attempts to bring before governments and the international community the continuing violations of people's freedom of religious association and organization. It sponsors development projects in the Third World and continues to organize international conferences—which are a common characteristic of these several streams of the inter-faith movement.

Temple of Understanding

The liberal optimism of the nineteenth century received a jarring setback in the twentieth. Within a few decades of the founding of these original inter-faith organizations, the Western world was shattered by two world wars, the death of over sixty million people, the loss of overseas colonies by European powers, the dangerous political polarization of the world through the emergence of two global superpowers, the threat of nuclear war, and the rise of militant nationalist movements. These developments combined to destroy the notion of an inexorable moral and spiritual evolution within human consciousness supported by the benign and enlightened use of technology. Liberalism in its nineteenth-century form died from a fatal dose of harsh reality. The period between the two world wars, therefore, was not a fertile one for inter-faith dialogue, as neo-conservative intellectual trends strongly influenced both the churches and universities.

With the dawn of the post-war era, however, things changed again. Threats to world peace posed by nuclear weapons brought millions of people into newly formed movements for peace and disarmament. A new spirit of internationalism arose in reaction to the violence of the century, spurred on by a growing global communications technology. And at the highest political levels, serious efforts were under way to create a global forum for international cooperation and peace called the United Nations.

While political negotiations for this were taking place, there arose a parallel notion for the creation of a spiritual United Nations, a place where the religions of the world could meet in council and fellowship. This idea had first occurred to a wealthy New England woman, Juliet Hollister, in the 1930s. She had in mind a physical building that could be a centre for spiritual wisdom and understanding. And she had a powerful friend. She enlisted the help of Eleanor Roosevelt.

Mrs. Hollister and Mrs. Roosevelt were a formidable duo. While their husbands were dealing with secular matters of state, they set about gathering support for their vision of a global spiritual centre. They visited the Pope, the Prime Minister of India, and Albert Schweitzer. They were encouraged to proceed. As others had done before them, they started with a series of meetings—"spiritual summits"—to which they invited the religious leaders of the world.

Mrs. Hollister's idea of a centre for world religions eventually acquired the name, Temple of Understanding. It has drawn together, since its inception in 1960, a distinguished array of internationally known scholars and secular leaders in a string of spiritual summit meetings held all over the world. It has moved towards the concept of "global spirituality"—a transcendent unity within the human family overcoming human divisions, but not negating differences of doctrine and belief.

The New York Conference of the Temple of Understanding in 1984 listed the following principles in the search for global spirituality:

1. The oneness of the human family
2. The place of the individual in the total order of things
3. The importance of spiritual exercises
4. The existence of conscience
5. The value of dedicated service to others
6. The duty to give thanks and express gratitude
7. The need for dialogue and action on world problems

8. The rejection of violence
9. An affirmation of love and compassion
10. Evolution toward an ever expanding realization of Divinity (*Pilgrimage of Hope*, 1992).

These noble ideals, which find resonance in the spiritual traditions of many faith communities, have shaped the focus and direction of the movement in the last decade. They emphasize the importance of belonging to a religious tradition and entering into its spiritual disciplines, the virtues of peaceful cooperation, a spirit of thanksgiving, and the ever-expanding horizon of a deeper knowledge of God to be gained through mutual understanding.

Though the dream of an actual building like the UN headquarters in New York and Geneva has never been realized, and is now abandoned as a priority, the Temple of Understanding has been influential in taking several international initiatives towards inter-faith collaboration at fairly high levels.

In particular, two organizations have grown from the parent body: the Global Forum and the North American Inter-Faith Network. The Global Forum exists to bring together politicians, scientists, journalists, artists, business leaders, and spiritual leaders to work on problems of human and environmental survival. These have involved major gatherings in recent years in Oxford, Moscow, Okayama, and Kyoto. The North American Inter-Faith Network, on the other hand, is a grassroots network of local and regional inter-faith groups in North America. Its purpose is to facilitate communication between local organizations and to encourage initiatives in community-building in multi-faith areas of the continent.

Both the Global Forum and the Network have had the considerable support of the Temple of Understanding, which is now located at the Episcopal Church's Cathedral of St. John the Divine in New York.

World Conference on Religion and Peace

It is estimated that by the end of the nineteenth century there were over four hundred organizations throughout the world committed to international peace. Some of them were connected with, and arose out of, the major world religions. But many were inspired by the values of humanism or non-religious philosophies. It was not long before the attempt was made to increase their effectiveness by uniting them together.

The World Conference on Religion and Peace (WCRP) has sought to highlight the ethical and political imperatives for peace promoted by both secular and religious movements, but in particular to harness the strength of the major religions to promote peace on a global scale. It has tried to link together the peace movements within each world religion and to make common cause with friendly and like-minded secular groups.

It began when the famous industrialist and philanthropist Andrew Carnegie called a distinguished group of American Catholic, Protestant, and Jewish leaders to his home in New York in 1914. Carnegie was a Scot who had been greatly dismayed in his youth by the violence of religious disputes. Under the influence of Swedenborg's teaching about "spiritual science," he developed a vision for world peace and planned to use his own position of power and wealth to promote the idea among religious leaders.

From this initiative there began in the same year the Church Peace Union— strangely titled, since it involved several Jews—which later became the WCRP. It was decided that the organization would have only individual members, rather than representatives of faith communities, to overcome the difficulty of finding official representation from those religions like Islam and Buddhism, which do not have central top-down structures.

Coincidentally, however, in 1914 the First World War began in Europe. Further development of Carnegie's vision was swept aside by the very thing he sought to prevent. The task was taken up again in 1928 when a conference in Geneva brought together Christians, Jews, Hindus, Buddhists, Confucians, Muslims, Baha'is, and followers of Shinto from Japan. The conference decided to "rouse and direct the religious impulses of humanity against war." But only a few years later, this hope was shattered again. Europe was convulsed for the second time in a generation, and this time the conflict spread to the Pacific.

Japan's attack on Pearl Harbor was a savage blow to the peace movement in Asia. It is perhaps surprising to many Westerners, but in the 1930s, in reaction to Japan's growing militarism and invasions of China and Korea—and before the attack on America—there had been persistent pressure for non-violence by several groups of people within Japan. A National Religious Conference for International Peace had been held in Tokyo as early as 1931, but like their European counterparts, Japanese pacifists were bitterly disappointed and marginalized within their own society by the events of the next few years.

After the Second World War, which was particularly disastrous for Japan because of the nuclear devastation of Hiroshima and Nagasaki, a much renewed and deeply committed peace movement began again. Japanese members became strong supporters of the WCRP and the first international conference was held in Kyoto in 1970. This led to the formation of a continuing international structure, with the office located in Tokyo.

Throughout the years since then, the WCRP has been highly critical of religious participation in war and violence, and has severely castigated the indifference shown by many believers to human suffering and environmental abuse. Speaking at a conference in Princeton in 1979, Catholic priest and writer Andrew Greeley critically attacked "selfish religious institutionalism, what I call even religious idolatry and chauvinism, that I see so prevalent in so many quarters in the contemporary scene. If we think national idolatry is bad, is not religious idolatry worse?" (*Pilgrimage of Hope,* 1992).

The capacity for self-criticism is a vital aspect of the renewal of any religious vision, and the WCRP has been a conscientious voice in calling for spiritual renewal in the cause of peace. Its efforts have focused on research into militarism, opposition to the proliferation of nuclear weapons, the promotion of disarmament, and consideration of the ethical dilemmas involved in the use of violence for the pursuit of justice.

The Melbourne conference in 1989 stated the focus of WCRP's philosophy in the form of four declarations:

1. We build trust through disarmament and through the strengthening of institutions for conflict resolution.
2. We build trust through the protection and preservation of human rights for all people.
3. We build trust by the creation of economic systems that provide for and assure the well-being of all and that conserve and respect the ecological balances of nature.

4. We build trust by educating ourselves and our children for peace, and through the use of non-violent methods of change and conflict resolution (*Pilgrimage of Hope*, 1992).

Unlike some of the other organizations in the inter-faith movement, therefore, which have a more personal or inward focus, the WCRP's aims are unapologetically social, economic, and political. They are assiduous in maintaining that the evils of the world cannot be overcome by prayer and heightened spiritual consciousness alone, but require the active involvement of believers in movements for political rights and social change. They engage themselves in the corporate and systemic aspects of religious activity, as well as the personal and interior.

The Melbourne event ended with a ringing summons to the hard path advocated by some of the great religious teachers of the world, from Buddha to Jesus to Gandhi: "Non-violence is love, and love is the most powerful force against injustice and violence."

Developments within the Christian Churches

Another stream that has contributed to the growing inter-faith movement throughout the world, and that has brought millions of Christians into new patterns of relationship with people of other religions during the latter half of this century, is the ecumenical movement. During the 1960s, when pressures were mounting for apparently inflexible and established institutions like churches to come to terms with modernity, significant changes were happening within the Protestant, Orthodox, Anglican, and Roman Catholic churches.

One of the catalysts for this was the Second Vatican Council, which had been called together under the leadership of Pope John XXIII, and was continued after his death by Pope Paul VI. This remarkable event was a watershed in modern religious history. Its roots and inspiration are complex, and cannot occupy us here, but among its many achievements was the *Declaration on the Relation of the Church to Non-Christian Religions*. In this statement, the Roman church declared "a sincere respect for those ways of acting and living, and those moral and doctrinal teachings ... which reflect the brightness of Truth" outside the Christian faith.

This marked a turning point in the relationship of the world's largest religious organization towards people of other traditions. We shall explore some of the theological implications of the declaration in Chapter 5, but its practical effects were immediate. A new openness—or *aggiornamento* (up-to-date-ness) as it was called—was encouraged among Catholics throughout the world, which unlocked the door for huge numbers of Christians to begin exploration of other spiritual paths.

Vatican II set the stage for large pilgrimages of Westerners, often young people, heading for Asia and seeking enlightenment and wisdom they could not find at home. Many notable Catholic priests were among them, venturing forth to establish new non-missionary relationships with other spiritual traditions. They included people like Thomas Merton, who began a well-publicized and promising dialogue with Buddhist monks, tragically cut short by his death in 1968, and Bede Griffiths, who established his own ashram in India, seeking ways to build bridges between Christians and Hindus through exploring common forms of prayer and spiritual discipline.

In October 1986, Pope John Paul II invited other world religious leaders to join him in the World Day of Prayer for Peace in the Italian town of Assisi, medieval home of the visionary St. Francis. Although this was not an occasion for new statements or official agreements, and it did not involve joint worship or any inter-faith celebration, it was nevertheless a profoundly significant sign to the world of the unity that can be found in prayer, and of the role of spiritual figures in offering a model of friendship and cooperation.

More slowly and with less cohesion than the Roman Catholic church, the World Council of Churches (WCC) began its discussions of world religions in 1971. A Sub-Unit on Dialogue Between Men of Living Faiths and Ideologies—now called the Dialogue with People of Living Faiths—was created in response to growing religious pluralism throughout the world and rising local tensions experienced by Protestant, Orthodox, and Anglican Christians.

The Nairobi Assembly of the WCC in 1975, however, revealed grave fault lines of disagreement among the member churches of the WCC on inter-faith questions. Evangelical Christians clashed with others on the issue of the uniqueness and absoluteness of Christ, and the place of other religions within God's plan of salvation. Similar problems arose in Vancouver in 1983 and Canberra in 1990, where fears of syncretism and paganism were raised by the presence of Australian Aboriginal participants and Christian feminists from Europe, North America, and Asia.

The World Council's most significant statement was issued after an ecumenical consultation at Baar, Switzerland, in 1990.

> We see the plurality of religious traditions as both the result of the manifold ways in which God has related to peoples and nations as well as a manifestation of the richness and diversity of humankind. We affirm that God has been present in their seeking and in their finding, that where there is truth and wisdom in their teachings, and love and holiness in their living ... this is the gift of the Holy Spirit. We also affirm that God is with them as they struggle, along with us, for justice and liberation.
>
> This conviction that God as creator of all is present and active in the plurality of religions makes it inconceivable to us that God's saving activity could be confined to any one continent, cultural type, or groups of peoples. A refusal to take seriously the many and diverse religious testimonies to be found among the nations and peoples of the whole world amounts to disowning the biblical testimony to God as creator of all things *(Ecumenical Press Service).*

The Baar Statement, however, has not yet been ratified by the WCC in any plenary assembly. It remains a conference communiqué of the participants.

Agreement has been difficult to find within the WCC membership of over three hundred autonomous national and regional churches. Its differences from the Roman Catholic structure, with the latter's centralized and authoritative magisterium, make comparison difficult and misleading. Nevertheless, religious pluralism is now firmly on the agenda of the WCC, and this is shaping a new modern climate of inter-faith awareness in many parts of the world.

Leading theological thinkers in the inter-faith field, such as Stanley Samartha and Wesley Ariarajah, have provided vital leadership within the WCC. Many international conferences have been held to further the goals of inter-faith cooperation, and to rethink traditional Christian mission in the light of history and modern experience. This work continues, albeit slowly, and progress is limited by the inherent diversity of the WCC, its function as a council of churches rather than an authoritative teaching body, as well as by current financial constraints.

The 1993 Parliament of the World's Religions

While the modern inter-faith movement began at the 1893 Parliament of the World's Religions, it was left to other groups to form continuing structures to keep the Chicago impetus going. The parliament itself was a single event, and its participants disbanded afterwards. It did not meet again until a hundred years later, to mark its centennial in 1993. But this later event was very different. The earlier conference had brought together less than a thousand participants; Chicago 1993 overwhelmed the organizers with over seven thousand registrations, almost double what had been expected. This number swelled to over ten thousand persons for the closing ceremony, at which the Dalai Lama was the principal speaker.

The second parliament was an indication both that the inter-faith movement now has a large and spirited group of adherents within many religious traditions, and also that the problems and difficulties of the movement remain profound. No attempt was made by the organizers to define what a "world religion" is, or to limit the participants to certain recognized faith groups. Consequently, the event attracted a number of new religious movements of sometimes dubious provenance, several "new age" cults, and even a group of self-proclaimed pagans. It therefore became difficult to focus any attention on the relationship among the major religions, and several of the sponsoring denominations withdrew their support and left the event shortly after it began.

The parliament was a smorgasbord of major plenary events, worship in a vast variety of styles, workshops conducted by hundreds of leaders on every topic imaginable, musical concerts, art displays, press conferences, outdoor celebrations, all-night vigils, and thousands of people in colourful, exotic robes pressed into often intense and sometimes humorous conversations in hallways and elevators. Over one hundred distinct religious groups were officially represented. This inclusivity was reflected in the plenary sessions, at which each day's theme was addressed by many different speakers, some of whom had never had such a global platform before.

The question I constantly asked myself—as one of the seven thousand attending—was whether this smorgasbord represented the genuine religious pluralism of modern society, or simply American cultural relativism. It was hard to imagine some of the participants who were given prominence by the organizers as seriously representing a global faith community. Some who were given the platform were obviously spiritual neophytes, captivated by the novelty of a single thought. But given the obvious difficulties in attempting to define who is and who is not a religious group, typical American fairness prevailed and no one was excluded.

This is not a normal pattern throughout the world in such gatherings. Though every religion—including Christianity—has at some point in its history been a new religious movement struggling for recognition, there is an argument to be made for restricting global conferences to truly global religions, and avoiding the confusion created by the presence of local or regional manifestations, such as the neo-pagan cults of Britain and North America. Failure to distinguish between religion and sect invites substantial and valid criticism of inter-faith endeavours.

Nevertheless, 1993 revealed considerable developments within the inter-faith movement since 1893. Where the earlier event had been dominated by Christians, who were in the great majority, its successor was notable for the absence of domination by one tradition. To this extent, the parliament did reflect successfully its goal, which was

> to promote understanding and cooperation among religious communities and institutions, to encourage the spirit of religious harmony and to celebrate, with openness and mutual respect, the rich diversity of religions, to assess and to renew the role of the religions of the world in relation to spiritual growth and to the critical issues and challenges facing the global community ... and to develop and encourage inter-faith groups and programs which will carry the spirit of the Parliament into the 21st century (*Parliament of the World's Religions*, 1993).

The major achievement of the parliament was the publication of the Declaration Towards a Global Ethic. It had been the hope of one of the main speakers of the parliament, distinguished Roman Catholic scholar Hans Küng, that the religions of the world might at last come together to make a common statement about the moral duties and obligations of the various traditions towards the well-being of humanity and the environment. Küng has made a substantial study in recent years of the ethical teachings of the world religions, and concludes that there is in each tradition an ethical core which shares similar characteristics with other religious teachings, and which can form the basis of a common moral imperative. The declaration is his attempt to construct a simple yet comprehensive statement of core values to which people of all religions can subscribe.

I have included the declaration in Appendix B because of its importance, not only as a statement of considerable merit in itself, but also as a sign of the convergence of the religious traditions around issues of common teaching and philosophy. It bears examination not simply for what it has to say about our contemporary human condition and the urgent spiritual response it calls forth from people of faith, but also because it is a helpful tool for pointing to common ethical values in the differing religions of the world.

I have often heard it said, for example, that Islam lacks an ethic, or that Hinduism is simply about the self and not the other. Christians have often laboured under the misapprehension that only Christ came to teach the world about love of neighbour. In fact, this reflects the polemics of inter-faith competition and not the reality of actual beliefs. Every developed spiritual tradition has had to come to terms with the horizontal dimension of person-to-person relationships, as well as the vertical dimension of the individual with the divine. Though each has its own doctrinal way of expressing these relationships and their consequent moral obligations, none of them lacks a fundamental commitment to human well-being and the demands of love and justice as necessary fruits of communion with God.

Küng's declaration was endorsed by a specially convened gathering of three hundred spiritual leaders at the 1993 parliament, and read to an attentive and deeply receptive crowd at the event's closing celebration. It has gone round the world since then and is being studied at many levels as a possible basis for some sort of United Nations commitment to global ethics, similar to other UN charters like the ones on human rights and the environment. There are inevitably criticisms and dissatisfactions, but the declaration in itself represents a substantial step forward in harnessing the cooperation of the world's religious peoples in a common effort for peace rather than for war.

A Promising Beginning

The first century of inter-faith exploration has come to an end. Its achievements have been limited but significant. The initial optimism of the movement, based on liberal and false assumptions of human progress, growing spiritual enlightenment, and harmonious international collaboration, has been replaced by a more practical realism, impelled by the worldwide threats of environmental crisis, ethnic warfare, and rising religious fundamentalism. The initial belief among some Christian visionaries of the late nineteenth century that the world would evolve towards Christianity through some natural spiritual law has given way to a genuine outlook of pluralism in which the continued existence of the world's religions is accepted as a given and as good.

Small inter-faith structures have come into being that provide venues for people of differing religions to meet, to engage in dialogue, to build community, and to work together on local or global projects. Though these various bodies do not have the kind of size, strength, or authority of the individual religions, they are earning growing respect as authentic expressions of the common spiritual voice of people of faith in pluralist societies. They represent the principal vehicles of cooperation and mutual understanding for those who are dissatisfied with the narrowness of religious orthodoxies and who are seeking means of interaction with spiritually diverse peoples.

These various bodies, briefly outlined here, all share certain characteristics. They are primarily gatherings of people rather than institutions. They meet in conferences and seminars all around the world, and then disband to meet again elsewhere. Many of the same people go to each other's events. They are largely, though not exclusively, formed from people at the liberal rather than the conservative end of their own doctrinal spectrum, though care needs to be taken here. Hinduism, for example, in its orthodox forms admits the existence of many paths to God, and Roman Catholicism in its most recent statements acknowledges the presence of God in other traditions; so inter-faith dialogue is now part of the mainstream orthodoxy in these and many traditions. Yet the movement attracts those with broader spiritual and doctrinal horizons.

The success of the 1993 parliament in Chicago in attracting huge crowds, and a large media corps of reporters and writers, suggests that the new post-Christian culture in the Western world is not entirely alienated from the traditional religions but is searching for new global expressions of spiritual truth grounded in the traditional paths. Both within the religions themselves, as well as among those who have abandoned traditional orthodoxies altogether, there is a desire for mutual cooperation and practical action to replace missionary competition. And there is also a new search for a global theology—not to replace the different religions but to comprehend them within a unifying vision. At its root this quest arises from the basic insight of all religious traditions, despite all their doctrinal precisions, of the fundamental and paradoxical inexpressibility of the divine.

Tensions remain deep, however. Those of us who witnessed the near brawl in Chicago in 1993 between Hindus and Sikh separatists over the future of Kashmir, when American security guards swooped into the plenary hall and closed the session for fear of violence, can be in no doubt about the complexities involved in dialogue where memories of mutual persecutions are still vivid and explosive. In situations of high conflict, it can be almost impossible to be in dialogue.

And there remains the question of theological truth. It is quite possible to be in relationship with people whom one believes to be fundamentally wrong, and many in the inter-faith movement continue to regard their fellow brothers and sisters as theologically or spiritually inferior, despite deliberate and honest efforts to be mutually respectful and tolerant. Often in fact—as in Chicago in 1993—the question of theological truth is intentionally not asked, for to enter the discussion at all is to risk division and to destroy harmony. And so people of varying outlooks are encouraged to come together simply for common action and statements, without any attempt to discriminate between authentic and inauthentic spiritual paths, and without the possibility of articulating a common vision of reality or a shared understanding of faith.

This difficulty in the field of inter-faith theology is systematically exploited by those within each faith tradition who oppose any accommodation or openness towards another faith tradition. And it is a difficulty that needs to be taken very seriously, for there are powerful arguments against inter-faith cooperation within every Western religion. There are those who believe that the truth of God has been definitively revealed and that obedience in faith demands an exclusive commitment to one's own religion rather than accommodation to the religion of others. Indeed, it appears to many Christians that such a view is mandated by the Bible and Christian tradition altogether.

Therefore, anyone who is engaged in the inter-faith movement, and wishes to be engaged with integrity and not simply for expediency, has to ask the question of religious truth. How can this openness to the differing spiritual paths of the world's peoples be compatible with the explicit truth claims and revelation of a particular historical religion? How can those who follow Christ accept the truth of any religion that rejects Christ? How can the command to preach the gospel to all nations (Matt. 28:19) be set aside for the sake of dialogue with those who believe another gospel?

It is to these questions we must now turn.

Chapter Four

Christian Exclusivism

*I*f Christianity is a true religion (indeed, *the* true religion), how can other religions be true as well? If Christians are to be faithful to the God of Scripture, the God who in Jesus declared, "I am the way, the truth, and the life. No one comes to the Father but by me" (John 14:6), how is it possible to be engaged in dialogue with those who must necessarily reject that declaration? And does participation in dialogue mean a surrender to relativism—the belief that truth, like beauty, is in the eye of the beholder, that it is merely an expression of personal preference?

Swami Vivekananda's pronouncement at the 1893 Parliament of the World's Religions that "all religions are true" has not been a position Christians have historically taken. Bishop Lesslie Newbigin, a missionary who spent much of his life in India, has observed that not all paths lead to the top of the mountain. Some lead over the precipice (*The Gospel in a Pluralist Society*, 1989).

How can one distinguish between true and false religions? Few people would want to argue that there is no such thing as a false belief. In Japan recently, a religious sect unleashed an attack of toxic gas on the Tokyo subway, killing several people. The sect had stockpiled enough gas to kill thousands of others. They had apparently developed a mindless loyalty to their charismatic leader, now under arrest in Japan. They were convinced they were being persecuted for holding the true vision about ultimate Reality. It is reminiscent of the Jonestown tragedy in the 1970s and the grisly deaths at Waco, Texas, in 1993, where other groups of devotees of a controlling leader fell under the grip of an apocalyptic doomsday vision leading to horror and death.

The participant in religious dialogue sooner or later must address the question of religious truth. This is not only because of the need to discriminate between healthy and unhealthy beliefs, but also because the claim to truth lies at the heart of each religion's self-understanding. If it is true, for example, that Jesus is the Messiah, the one predicted in the Hebrew Scriptures, how can it also be true—as Jews still believe—that the Messiah is yet to come? Or again, if it is true, as Muslims believe, that the Koran replaces and supersedes the revelations given through Moses and Jesus, how can it also be true, in the words of the Bhagavad Gita, that "I am in every religion as the thread through a string of pearls"? The fact is, the world's religious doctrines are often mutually contradictory, and cannot be reconciled into intellectual compatibility without the kind of revisionism each of them would deny.

The advent of the modern inter-faith movement has stirred up quite a controversy among Christian thinkers and theologians. It has led some of them to defend with even greater rigour the traditional Christian claim to possess the final truth about God. It has led others to explore ways of retaining Christian superiority without negating entirely the truth claims of other religions. And it has led some to sever the connection with traditional Christian orthodoxy—as John Hick puts it, to "cross the Rubicon" of faith—and propose a new global theology.

Theological attitudes undergird every approach to inter-religious dialogue. If one believes that all religions are true, then one approaches dialogue with the expectation of encountering God in and through the other. One naturally adopts an attitude of humility and openness since it is an *a priori* assumption that everyone has something to learn, that all may deepen their knowledge of the living God.

If, on the other hand, one believes the Hindu, the Buddhist, the Muslim, and so on, to be a heathen and a pagan, mired in error and lost in darkness, then the opposite attitude will prevail. One might well adopt a posture of charity and compassion towards the other, even a tolerant kindness, since those who reject truth in other religions do not necessarily resort to violence against them, but there will be no expectation of encountering afresh God's truth, no hope of expanding the horizons of spiritual understanding.

In Christian theology, three general positions can be described with respect to other religions. These are widely named today as exclusivism, inclusivism, and pluralism. In this and the next two chapters, I will describe these positions briefly and indicate both the strengths and weaknesses of each of them. While some are obviously more promising than others for the field of inter-faith dialogue, I want to stress that no position is without its difficulties. None is completely "right" from a theological point of view and none, perhaps, completely wrong. And though we cannot and should not avoid the struggle for theological clarity, we should also be warned that theology by itself can never bring about agreement on the question of truth.

Exclusivism

Exclusivism is the position which holds that such truth as can be known about God has been fully revealed in Jesus Christ. While it is recognized that human knowledge of God is only partial (1 Cor. 13:12), nevertheless Christ is the one in whom the fullness of God's being came to dwell (John 1:14), to whom all things in heaven and on earth are subject (Col. 1:16), without whom no one may come to the knowledge of God (John 14:6), and at whose name every knee shall bow when the universal day of judgement comes (Phil. 2:10).

Exclusivism is based on the belief that Jesus Christ is the final and complete revelation of God, and that he represents an absolute point of faith from which no true Christian can depart. Human salvation has been won by Christ on the cross, and by him alone. There is no other name by which we may be saved (Acts 4:12). Faith in his atoning death and redemptive resurrection is the only path to eternal life. There cannot therefore be many paths to God, for it is this particular path that has been opened up for us by God himself. This "scandal of particularity" may be folly to the non-believing world, a stumbling block to Christianity's intellectual credibility, but it is the wisdom of God (1 Cor. 1:24). This wisdom, and no other, is the one Christians are given the power and freedom to proclaim. The uniqueness of Christ is an absolute requirement for faith, and to question it is to deny orthodox Christian belief and to court the very heresies the New Testament repudiates.

This is clearly the oldest and most established Christian position. It is rooted in certain passages of Scripture, and in some early Christian traditions. It has shaped centuries of Christian reflection on interfaith encounter, and has become enshrined in certain teachings of the church down through the ages. This view of the absoluteness of Christianity has clear implications for attitudes to people outside the church. It was expressed directly and without compromise, for example, by the Council of Florence in 1438: "No one remaining outside the Catholic Church, not just pagans, but also Jews or heretics or schismatics, can become partakers of eternal life; but they will go to the everlasting fire which was prepared for the devil and his angels, unless before the end of life they are joined to the Church."

This theological sentiment undergirded the Inquisition, that period from the thirteenth to the nineteenth century in Europe in which the Roman Catholic church sought to establish uniformity of doctrine throughout its dominion by prosecuting false teaching and unbelief. Though the statement sounds harsh to modern ears, and its application was frequently brutal and cruel, its advocates believed it to be a compassionate teaching. Love of neighbour and concern for the immortal soul of each human being prompted the evangelistic correction of false beliefs—sometimes even aggressively—for it was the desire of the church that no one should be lost to the everlasting fire that awaited the unbelieving.

It is important to note that the warning contained in the declaration from Florence is directed not only at non-Christians, but also at heretics and schismatics, that is, Christians who do not follow the official teachings of the established church. All are lumped together—Jews, and pagans, reformers and dissenters within the church—and, placed under dire threat of eternal punishment in torment unless they return to the fold. This, therefore, was not a teaching directed solely at people of other religions. Its practical effect, however, was to legitimize discrimination and barbarism towards the non-Christian peoples of the world, all the more so when it became linked with militarism and colonialism after the fifteenth century.

The teaching of the Council of Florence is now known by the Latin phrase *extra ecclesiam nulla salus;* "outside the church no salvation." It provided the theological basis for mission and evangelism throughout the world. It was believed to be the direct consequence of the instruction of Jesus to the disciples in Matthew's gospel: "Go therefore and make disciples of all nations, baptizing them in the name of the Father, and of the Son, and of the Holy Spirit" (28:19). And it offered to Christian believers the assurance of salvation, giving them confidence to act in the name of God in all endeavours undertaken in the service of the church.

The Florence statement is classically Roman in its construction. Roman Catholic theology has always emphasized the importance of belonging to the *church.* It is the church, in this view, that as the body of Christ is the mediator of salvation to the world. Accordingly, the important thing is to be within the fold, to belong and be recognized by the religious community. In Catholic tradition, this has often outweighed the importance of personal belief and faith in Jesus Christ.

Protestant tradition has leaned in the opposite direction. As the medieval church arrogated to itself certain powers and privileges that were far from the example of Christ, and that could not be justified from apostolic teaching in Scripture, Protestant Reformers emphasized the once-for-all character of Christ's redemption on the cross, and the personal inward acceptance of his offer of salvation, as the normative and central elements of Christian belief, rather than acquiescence in the teachings of the magisterium.

This leads to another kind of exclusivism, however, only in a Protestant form. And it is not limited to a period in medieval or Renaissance history. In this century, the Lausanne Declaration expresses this view:

> There is only one Redeemer and only one Gospel ... We repudiate as a slight on Jesus Christ and the Gospel any syncretism and any dialogue which claims that Jesus Christ speaks equally through all religions and ideologies. Jesus Christ, true man and true God, gave himself as the sole

redemption for sinners. He is the only mediator between God and man. And there is no other name by which we are saved. All men and women are lost in their sin. But God loves everyone. He does not will that anyone should be lost, but that everyone should repent. However, those who reject Jesus Christ scorn the joy of salvation and thus condemn themselves to eternal separation from God (*Lausanne Declaration,* 1974).

This position differs from Florence in two respects. First, while Florence took the view that there is no salvation outside the church, Lausanne holds that there is no salvation outside a personal and explicit confession of faith in Jesus Christ. Lausanne, in keeping with conservative Protestant tradition, denies the view that divine grace is given through membership in the corporate body of the church itself. Rather, grace is received only through individual faith. This is a watershed criterion along which much Christian theology and practice has been divided.

Lausanne does emphasize the universality of God's love, which is withheld from no one, but at the same time holds to the particularity of salvation through Christ alone. Therefore the task of Christian mission is to reach everyone with the preaching of this gospel, to attempt to convert every human being to Christ, and so to participate in the liberation of the whole world from the power of sin and death, which is available through this means alone.

Second, Lausanne speaks only of "eternal separation" from God as the consequence of wilful rebellion against Christ. Florence was more explicit, warning of the pain and agony of the burning fire prepared for the devil and all his angels. Exclusivists differ from each other on this point, with some reluctant to pronounce on the exact nature of the afterlife for the damned, preferring the gentler scenario of separation, oblivion, or simply missing out on the rewards of righteousness. But others have no hesitation in predicting the dramatic effects of unbelief. Thus the Congress on World Mission, a conference of Protestant evangelicals meeting in Chicago in 1960, declared that "in the years since the war, more than one billion souls have passed into eternity and more than half of these went to the torment of hell fire without even hearing of Jesus Christ, who He was, or why He died on the cross of Calvary" (John Hick and Brian Hebblethwaite, *Christianity and Other Religions*, 1980).

The urgency of this situation, with more than a billion souls lost because they have not had the gospel preached to them, is presented as a tragedy of such dimensions as to galvanize renewed efforts at world evangelization and conversion. Salvation, in this theology, is available only to individuals who respond to Jesus Christ with repentance and faith. It cannot be dispensed by the church. And it cannot be found through any other religion.

Exclusivism is found in many religious traditions, not simply in Christianity. There are Hindu forms of it in India, for instance, where in some states conversion from Hinduism to another religion is forbidden by law. In Indonesia, the world's largest Muslim country, Sharia law makes it illegal to attempt to convert people away from Islam, though the practice of Christianity by Christians is permitted. In Pakistan, even this tolerance is observed as much in the breach as in the keeping of it, especially by local mullahs, and Christians are severely persecuted in this and other countries by the process of Islamicization, which makes public Christian witness an act of blasphemy. And certain expressions of Judaism, especially in Israel, zealously guard the religious integrity of the state by opposing the privileges given to other faith traditions.

In Christianity, theological exclusivism is most closely associated with the conservative evangelical tradition within Protestantism. This tradition upholds the Bible as the supreme authority for Christian life and doctrine, accepts the verbal inspiration and inerrancy of Scripture, rejects any theological development that waters down or relativizes traditional beliefs, maintains the literal truth of such doctrines as the virgin birth, the bodily resurrection, and the visible return of Jesus, and affirms the uniqueness of Jesus Christ in such a way as to make him the absolute condition for salvation.

Within North America there is a resurgence of strength among conservative evangelicals as the culture searches for foundations and values in a post-modern age. One of the intellectual leaders of this movement is James Packer of Regent College in Vancouver. In a recent paper given in Montreal, Packer argues for exclusivism as the firm foundation for Christian evangelism in the 1990s:

We are obligated in practice to evangelize on the basis that there is no salvation for anyone whom we encounter apart from faith in Christ.

If we cannot be confident that there would have been any hope for us had we not learned of Christ and been brought to personal faith in him, we have no basis for holding out such hope in the case of anyone else, however strongly charity prompts us to want to do so.

Inclusivist speculation about salvation for the unevangelized is thus necessarily unfruitful, and is likely to distract us from our present witnessing task (*Jesus Christ the Only Saviour*, 1994).

The nuance in this passage is interesting, and even somewhat encouraging, since it avoids any categorical denial of hope for the "unevangelized." It merely states that Christians have no knowledge of such a possibility. It is outside the realm of revealed truth in Scripture. Packer appears, in this sense, to be agnostic about the prospect of salvation for others, rather than contemptuous of it. But he stands firm in maintaining, in the absence of any other theological conviction—and against even the promptings of charity—that salvation by faith in Christ alone is non-negotiable.

The Essentials '94 conference in Montreal incorporated this position into its final statement. Called the Montreal Declaration of Anglican Essentials, it confirms the evangelical position of Lausanne in Article 4, entitled "The Only Saviour":

Human sin is prideful rebellion against God's authority, expressing itself in our refusing to love both the Creator and his creatures. Sin co-opts our nature, and its fruit is injustice, oppression, personal and social disintegration, alienation and guilt before God; it destroys hope and leads to a future devoid of any enjoyment of either God or good. From the guilt, shame, power, and path of sin, Jesus Christ is the only Saviour. Penitent faith in him is the only way of salvation (George Egerton, *Anglican Essentials*, 1995).

Exclusivism has certain strengths and weaknesses from a theological point of view. It can appeal to many passages in Scripture for authority and support. For example:

I am the way, and the truth, and the life. No one comes to the Father except through me (John 14:6).

There is salvation in no one else, for there is no other name under heaven given among mortals by which we must be saved (Acts 4:12).

Therefore God also highly exalted him and gave him the name that is above every name, so that at the name of Jesus every knee should bend, in heaven and on earth and under the earth (Phil. 2:9–10).

For there is one God; there is also one mediator between God and humankind, Christ Jesus (1 Tim. 2:5).

Those who believe in him are not condemned; but those who do not believe are condemned already, because they have not believed in the name of the only Son of God (John 3:18).

For Christians these passages are important, since the Bible is the primary ground in our tradition for the divine revelation in Christ. It is through Scripture that we are led to Christ, and through Christ to God. These texts, then, appear to give compelling force to historic Christian attitudes towards other religions.

There is also powerful motivation here for Christian mission and evangelism, for building up the church and reaching out to the world with the message of Christ. If you take seriously the command of Jesus to love your neighbour, and if you believe your neighbour has but one opportunity to find eternal life and you yourself have been given the responsibility to warn them of it, you are not likely to be complacent about approaching him or her with the good news of the gospel. In a society such as ours, which is publicly and officially silent about religious truth, though extraordinarily loud about things of no consequence at all, this kind of Christian activism has much to commend it.

Such approaches need not necessarily be invasive nor even unwelcome. If the real alternative to Christian faith for a particular person is not another established religious path, but rather drugs, alcohol, sex, or money, there is no doubt which is the better option. The evangelistically committed believer may sometimes be more useful in these situations as an agent of genuine healing than one who takes the view that all paths lead to God.

However, there are fatal weaknesses in exclusivism, both in its interpretation of Scripture and more particularly in its doctrine of God. With its commitment to the inerrancy of Scripture, exclusivist theology treats the Bible solely as divine revelation and disregards its context as a product of human history. A great deal of recent biblical scholarship has attempted to uncover both the confessional and the historical basis of the sayings attributed in the Bible to Jesus, and there is reason today to doubt whether some of the exclusivist pronouncements we find on the lips of our Lord were actually said by him.

Much light has been shed in recent years by biblical scholars on how the books of the New Testament came to be written down. There are evident differences, and even serious discrepancies, among the four gospels in their accounts of the life of Jesus. The popular theory that they are straight historical and biographical reports, as one might read today of some famous person, has long been discarded. It cannot explain how some material appears commonly in some of the accounts while certain material is particular to each account and does not appear elsewhere.

The view has now widely evolved that each of the gospels is the product of a particular Christian community. Each gospel has been shaped according to particular theological emphases and current experiences, and presents a unique aspect of the life of Jesus that is nuanced and differentiated from one gospel to another. The implications of this for modern biblical understanding are enormous.

For example, perhaps the most clearly absolutist pronouncements uttered by Jesus occur in the last gospel, the Gospel of John. Scholars are generally agreed that this was written towards the end of the first century of the Christian Era, some sixty years or so after the death of Jesus. By this time in the early Christian community two things were happening. The church was experiencing increasing conflict with the Jewish religion from which it had sprung, and also it was moving out into the Gentile world of Hellenistic syncretism where it sought to establish Christian faith in the face of a marketplace of alternative beliefs and spiritualities.

John's gospel was written by and for a Jewish-Christian community experiencing the shock of persecution and rejection. The Johannine church had been expelled from the synagogue. Its message of the fulfilment of Jewish messianic expectation in Jesus Christ was no longer acceptable. There may even have been violent attacks on the fledgling movement by Jewish gangs (John 16:2). When it came to write down the story of Jesus, the Johannine community was clearly influenced by these events, and looked for ways to understand them in the light of who Jesus was believed to be.

It is only in John's gospel that we find such statements as "he who does not honour the Son does not honour the Father who sent him" (5:23); and "you are of your father the devil, and your will is to do your father's desires. He was a murderer from the beginning and has nothing to do with the truth" (8:44). It is in this gospel alone that we find the statements on the lips of Jesus, "I and the Father are one. He who has seen me has seen the Father" (10:30 and 14:9); and "No one comes to the Father except through me" (14:6). And it is only in this gospel that strongly worded barbs against Jews as such are made. It is "the Jews" who are held responsible for Christ's crucifixion, and "the Jews" who called for the release of Barabbas (in the other gospels it is "the crowd").

We must attempt to give some account of this. It is not sufficient simply to claim that this is fact and must have happened as reported. It may be that the denial of Jesus by the synagogue Jews led to a heightened emphasis on his messiahship and supremacy by the Johannine Jews. Certainly, there is a disturbing connection in the fourth gospel between the glorification of Jesus on the one hand and anti-Jewish polemic on the other. This has been the focus of much recent study as a root cause of historic Christian anti-Semitism. German theologian Reinhold Bernhardt comments,

> The Johannine community reacted to the acute threat from outside by making its own conviction absolute. The sharp statements which thus arose are to be interpreted as a reaction to a quite specific challenge and not as universal suprahistorical judgments on the religions of the world. They cannot simply be transferred to quite different situations ... Where the background to the polemic no longer exists, the polemic no longer has any justification (*Christianity Without Absolutes*, 1994).

Bernhardt goes on to argue that the other New Testament statements that offer apparent rejection of other religions are to be understood in this same light. The tendency of exclusivists to regard them as absolute statements relating to other world religions in effect de-historicizes Scripture and attempts to apply particular verses to situations for which they were never intended. What we do know from the New Testament, and especially from the earlier gospels and letters, is that in his life and ministry Jesus appears to have been a faithful Jew, and that his teachings and example point in the opposite direction to a narrow exclusivism.

> Jesus was aware of having been sent to the Jews (Matt.15:24), and he also sent his disciples to the Jews (Matt. 10:5). So he had no occasion to argue with the non-Jewish religions and their gods as such. But in his behaviour he made no distinction in principle between Jews and non-Jews. He even presented non-Jews, pagans, as models of faith, like the Canaanite (Syro-Phoenician) woman whose daughter he healed (Matt. 15:21–28), or the (Roman) centurion of Capernaum who asked for help for his sick servant (Matt. 8:5–13).

> When Jesus sat by the Samaritan woman at the well and even spent two days in her village (John 4), he was breaking a tabu: it was forbidden to Jews to have contact with the despised Samaritans. Furthermore, in the parable of the good Samaritan he presented the Jews with a man from Samaria whom they regarded as godless in the function of an unselfish helper (Luke 10: 29–37).

> Jesus was indifferent to religious and social barriers where the salvation of men and women was at stake. Perhaps he even had no occasion to engage in argument with non-Jewish religions and their gods because he knew that pagans, like Jews, were ultimately included in God's all-embracing will for salvation (*Christianity Without Absolutes*, 1994).

So the texts that appear to support the exclusivist view do so only when extracted from their local context and isolated by elevation into global doctrines. Such a position can only be maintained by separating the texts from their historical setting, a method biblical scholars today generally avoid. Christians who take quite different positions with respect to other religions can also in fact claim biblical support, as we shall see. The exclusivist assurance that the Bible supports only one position with respect to other religious paths begins to dissolve under examination.

Perhaps even more problematic than this de-historicizing of Scripture is the doctrine of God on which its foundations rest. The notion that a billion souls have gone down to the torment of hell fire without even hearing of Jesus Christ is not only repugnant and abhorrent, it also implies a God who is repugnant and abhorrent. That God should actually condemn everyone who is not joined to the church to an eternity of everlasting fire defies all moral sense and contradicts everything we know about God, both from the witness of Scripture and from the life of Jesus.

If we took it to be true, it would mean that God condemns the vast majority of the world's peoples to a hopeless and brutal destiny. It would mean believing in a God who goes to the trouble of creating all human beings in the divine image and then offers salvation only to a small fraction of them, the ones who happen to be Christians. It would suggest that all humanity existing before Jesus Christ, and those who have lived afterwards out of reach of the Christian gospel, as well as those who for various reasons have not understood or have not had sufficient reason to be convinced of the truth of Christ on account of its all too fallible ambassadors, are all alike condemned to final damnation, while those whose good fortune has placed them in the church, whether by accident or by birth, reap the benefits of everlasting joy.

The problem with exclusivism is that it presents us with a god from whom we need to be delivered rather than the living God who is the hope of the world. The exclusivist god is narrow, rigid, and blind. This god pays no attention to the sanctity and personal holiness of people outside the Christian fold. This god takes no loving and parental pride in the lives of great spiritual teachers who spoke of other paths to truth, figures like Moses, Siddartha, Mohammed, and Gandhi, as well as ordinary people like my Hindu hosts in Bombay. This god is compassionate only towards Christians (and, if we are honest, only to certain kinds of Christians) and is obsessed with the conviction that everyone in the world must become like these Christians or else they will be forever cursed.

Such a god is not worthy of honour, glory, worship, or praise. This god offers no hope for a world deeply divided along religious lines, a world crying out for peace and reconciliation. This theology truncates and diminishes the universality and majesty of the true and living God, who is known in every nation but by many names. It compromises the mercy and love of God by ascribing elitist and restrictive doctrines of salvation to the One whom Jesus described as caring for every sparrow that falls to the ground. And it forces us into the unwanted and unnecessary position of choosing either to abandon belief in the God who creates all and loves all even beyond death, or to abandon those outside the Christian faith to a hopeless and tragic destiny.

Exclusivism excludes—this is the difficulty. It leads to a morally and spiritually intolerable gospel, to a god who plays favourites with his children. It takes us far away from the loving God of Jesus' parables, the God who welcomes home the prodigal son, the God who pays the latecomers to the vineyard the same wages as those who have worked all day. The god of exclusivism is an idol.

For these reasons, many Christians have abandoned the position advocated by the Council of Florence, and most recently by Protestant evangelicals. They have moved to a second position, which can be called inclusivism.

Chapter Five

Christian
Inclusivism

*I*nclusivist theology attempts to hold together two biblical principles that on the surface appear to be contradictory. One is that God makes possible the salvation of all people. The second is that salvation is through Christ alone.

Like the exclusivist position, this one also takes very seriously the authority of Scripture for Christian belief, but it is more open to the world of religious faith in its manifold variety and more faithful to the images of God presented in the Bible. It acknowledges those many biblical passages that declare God's saving health among all nations and God's desire for the well-being of all humankind. For example:

> And all the ends of the earth shall see the salvation of our God (Isa. 52:10).

> Let the nations be glad and sing for joy, for you judge the peoples with equity and guide the nations upon earth (Ps. 67:4).

In past generations he allowed all the nations to follow their own ways; yet he has not left himself without witnesses in doing good—giving you rains from heaven and fruitful seasons, and filling you with food and your hearts with joy (Acts 14:16–17).

This is right and is acceptable in the sight of God our Saviour, who desires everyone to be saved and to come to the knowledge of the truth (1 Tim. 2:4).

For he will repay according to each one's deeds: to those who by patiently doing good seek for glory and honour and immortality, he will give eternal life; there will be glory and honour and peace for everyone who does good, the Jew first and also the Greek. For God has no favourites (Rom. 2:7–11).

I have other sheep that do not belong to this fold. I must bring them also, and they will listen to my voice (John 10:16).

It is clear from Scripture that God desires the fulfilment of the entire creation, and that there is no partiality or favouritism shown to any particular religious group. Not even the Hebrews, as God's chosen people, were promised salvation to the exclusion of all others, nor were they to be spared judgement or suffering. In fact, God's choice of the Hebrews as a covenant people was intended to set them apart as a special example to the world, a sign to all the world's peoples, of the universality of God's love and justice. God was not their special property, but they were to be God's light, a light that would illuminate God's witnesses in every part of the earth.

Within the Christian church, it was Paul who first struggled with the question of salvation outside Hebrew religion. It was an important theological question for the church in the first century as Jewish-Christians began to proclaim the gospel beyond Palestine. In Romans 1 through 4, Paul addresses the question of whether salvation is possible for those who are not believers. Here the great apostle of justification by faith deliberately rejects the notion that Jews who lived before Christ cannot be saved. He considers the life of Abraham and the example of David, and argues that these found favour in the sight of God because of their faith.

Now obviously, theirs was not faith in Jesus Christ since they had lived centuries before him. It was their love of God that was counted as righteousness, and this is true, Paul argues, for Gentiles also. Though not of our faith, he says, they have nevertheless been given the knowledge of God. God searches the human heart and conscience to see what is written there.

> To those who by patiently doing good seek for glory and honour and immortality, he will give eternal life ... there will be anguish and distress for everyone who does evil ... but glory and honour and peace for everyone who does good, the Jew first and also the Gentile. For God has no favourites (Rom. 2:7–11).

Those who have lived before Christ, and those who have lived outside the sphere of the law of Moses, will not be condemned because they lacked faith in Christ. They will be the recipients of the same impartiality with which God looks upon all the faithful. It is human conduct, not credal belief, that God rewards. Paul makes the important statement that God has no favourites, and then ends his argument with the assertion that "on that day, according to my gospel, God, through Jesus Christ, will judge the secret thoughts of all " (Rom. 2:16).

Here is the second part of the inclusivist equation. Salvation is possible for those outside the realm of faith—but God's judgement will nevertheless be exercised through Jesus Christ; that is, according to the truth revealed in him alone. This means that salvation is possible for everyone precisely because of Christ's sacrificial atonement for the sins of the whole world. In Christ, God was reconciling the whole world to himself (Col. 1:20; 2 Cor 5:19). Christ's salvation therefore is not simply for those who believe in him, but also for those who do not know him, yet who yearn after God in their lives and seek to act with love and justice.

Building on this argument in Romans, inclusivist theology contends that people do not need to become Christian in order to inherit the fruits of Christ's redemption. Salvation is open to all human beings through whatever spiritual path has been given to them. Inclusivism recognizes and corrects the problems associated with the exclusivist view of other religions, namely the doctrine of God exclusivist tradition implies.

It is obviously intolerable to believe in a God who consigns to hell or oblivion those who are not Christian and yet lead exemplary, just, and holy lives, or attempt to do so. There is recognition here that the damnation of millions who lived before Christ, and of billions who have lived after him and have not accepted faith in him, points to an unjust God who is arbitrary and callous. The promptings of charity have been given a hearing now, and we have a truly biblical doctrine of God, whose compassion and mercy are universal, whose love is predominant, and where—in the words of the old hymn— "there's a wideness in God's mercy, like the wideness of the sea."

The clearest expression of the inclusivist position is to be found in the recent teaching of the Roman Catholic church. The Second Vatican Council's *Declaration on the Relation of the Church to Non-Christian Religions,* issued in 1965, takes a very different position from the earlier Council of Florence.

> The Catholic Church rejects nothing which is true and holy in these religions. She has a sincere respect for those ways of acting and living, those moral and doctrinal teachings which may differ in many respects from what she holds and teaches, but which none the less reflect the brightness of that Truth which is the light of all men. But she proclaims, and is bound to proclaim unceasingly, Christ, who is "the way, the truth and the life" (John 14:6). In him men find the fullness of their religious life and in him God has reconciled all things to himself (2 Corinthians 5:18).

This position allows for a partial, if incomplete, measure of truth in the other religions of the world. It maintains the historic position of the church that the fullness of God's light is revealed only in Jesus Christ, and yet it also rejoices that the light of his truth shines beyond the church and into the religious lives of other people. It takes the forward step of recognizing that God may be known in other ways and encountered along paths other than the one Christians know. Yet it stops far short of conceding to others any ultimate knowledge of God. The church alone, in this statement, remains its sole possessor. And it says nothing about salvation beyond the church. Carefully and with masterful precision, Vatican II never actually repudiates anything in the Council of Florence. Without denying that there is no salvation outside the church, it simply calls for openness, dialogue, fellowship, and mutual respect among the world's religious peoples. This remains the position of the Roman Catholic church today.

Theologically, however, the question remains whether this new respect for people of other religions can extend to the possibility of salvation for those who reject Christ. This issue has occupied much thought among Roman Catholic theologians. Before Vatican II, important efforts were made to build a theological foundation for a thoroughgoing salvific inclusivism that did not depart from the teaching of the church. The most notable of these was a lecture in 1961 by the German scholar Karl Rahner, in which he invented the notion of the "anonymous Christian."

> God desires the salvation of everyone. And this salvation willed by God is the salvation won by Christ ... It is a salvation really intended for all those millions upon millions of people who lived perhaps a million years before Christ—and also for those who have lived after Christ—in nations, cultures and epochs of a very wide range.

> If it is true that a person who ... may already be on the way to his salvation, and someone who in certain circumstances finds it, without being reached by the proclamation of the Church's message—and if it is at the same time true that this salvation which reaches him in this way is Christ's salvation, since there is no other salvation—then it must be possible to be ... an anonymous Christian.

> The proclamation of the Gospel does not simply turn someone absolutely abandoned by God and Christ into a Christian, but turns an anonymous Christian into someone who now also knows about his Christian belief (*Christianity and the Non-Christian Religions*, 1961).

This is a rather novel idea, and on the face of it holds some promise for those who wish to remain faithful to the biblical proclamation of salvation through Christ alone and who also wish to see the sphere of God's redemption include all people of faith and good will. Rahner suggests that a person living outside the church, who leads an exemplary life and desires to know God, is redeemed by Christ on the cross even though this person is incapable of knowing it. He suggests the possibility that all who are saved are in fact saved by Christ alone, but that knowledge of the fact is not necessary for the recipient of it. Those who are saved are saved by Jesus Christ, whether they know it or not. Salvation therefore is not limited to Christians. Yet only Christians fully know its true dimensions, and how it has been won.

This is, of course, a major departure from the conservative Protestant insistence on personal faith and repentance, and so has never commanded much respect from that quarter. But within Catholic tradition it has received some attention. It was a revolutionary new concept, and opened up some creative ground for accommodation and openness.

Rahner was attempting to build on Paul's argument in Acts 17, where we find the notion of the "unknown god." Paul had gone up to the Areopagus in Athens to debate with the philosophers there. He pointed to the shrines marked with the many divine names of the Greek pantheon, and then noticed one without a name, a shrine to the unknown god. In the Greek syncretistic tradition, this was a way of acknowledging that there is always more to learn about the divine, always an unknown quality that may yet be revealed in some new way. Paul argued that the name of this god was now known: it had been revealed in Christ. There was no longer any reason to look for other gods, but through repentance and forgiveness of sins, one could seek redemption of the one true God of whom Paul was an ambassador.

This passage is often presented by adherents of the exclusivist school as further grounds for rejection of other religions. But in fact, it is a model of dialogical engagement. What was being debated was not the issue of the salvation of non-Christians, but the merits of monotheism over polytheism, which was the Greek belief at the time, and the possibility of knowledge of the one true God. The question of whether there is one god or many is not a question in current inter-faith dialogue. Rather, with the exception of the special case of non-theistic Buddhism, the great religions of the world believe in a single divine Creator. Rahner's adaptation of this biblical argument to the context of modern religious pluralism is intended essentially to safeguard the same point.

In response to the obvious objection that there is an inherent presumption in the inclusivist argument, that it still maintains the superiority of Christianity over other religions albeit within a veiled comprehensiveness, Rahner writes,

> Non-Christians may think it presumption for the Christian to regard the non-Christian as a Christian who has not yet come to himself reflectively. But the Christian cannot renounce this

"presumption" which is really the source of the greatest humility. For it is a profound admission that God is greater than man and the Church.

The Church is not the communion of those who possess God's grace as opposed to those who lack it, but is the communion of those who can explicitly confess what they and the others hope to be (*Christianity and the Non-Christian Religions*, 1961).

Another similar attempt along these same lines has been made by the Indian Roman Catholic theologian Raimundo Panikkar. In 1968, shortly after Vatican II's admission that the light of Christ shines in the faith of the world's peoples, Panikkar pondered the possibility of an evolving consciousness towards Christ in the other religions of the world. He was most familiar with the religion of his native country, India. In an essay entitled "The Unknown Christ of Hinduism," he suggested that the presence of Christ might be discerned within Hinduism by those outside that tradition but sympathetic towards it.

We all meet in God. God is not only everywhere, but everything is in Him, and we, including all our strivings and actions, are of Him, in Him, from Him, to Him.

Now, there is only one link, one mediator between God and the rest. That is Christ, from whom everything has come, in whom everything subsists, to whom everything that shall endure the bite of time will come.

Hence, for Christianity, Christ is already there in Hinduism in so far as Hinduism is a true religion; Christ is already at work in any Hindu prayer as far as it is really prayer; Christ is behind any form of worship, in as much as it is adoration made to God.

That Christ which is already in Hinduism ... has not yet unveiled his whole face, has not yet completed his whole mission there. He still has to grow up and be recognized ... Hinduism is not yet his spouse (*The Unknown Christ of Hinduism*, 1968).

There is a wonderful flavour of Hindu universalism in this approach: that sense of God being the ocean in which all streams meet, the Omega point (to use Teilhard de Chardin's phrase) to which all human strivings tend, the utterly transcendent Reality that relativizes our human efforts at spiritual understanding and yet gathers them all together. There is a suggestion also of the unfinished character of religion, its essential incompleteness, which cannot be otherwise until we meet God face to face at the final moment of truth's unveiling.

Inclusivism, as expressed by these different exponents, varies in its emphasis and detail. There is an implicit distinction between the faith of the individual and the religion to which one belongs. Inclusivists tend to argue that, outside the Christian community, the grace of God acts through persons rather than religions. Rahner believes that God can and does bring non-Christians into the kingdom of heaven, but through the merit of their good intentions rather than through the doctrines and spiritual disciplines of their beliefs. Panikkar, on the other hand, believes that God works through other religions as well, though incompletely. But both are agreed that Christ is the only Saviour, and that only Christians have the benefit of knowing this.

In the end, the Second Vatican Council did not utilize any theory of "anonymous Christianity" in its 1965 declaration. It treated the theories as speculations, attempts to extend Christology into the field of inter-faith dialogue in an exploratory way. The declaration itself offers no theology of world religions. It is primarily a pastoral document, an attempt to get beyond the bitterness and rivalry of inter-religious hostility. To that extent, however, it was a remarkable advance.

The strength of the inclusivist position is its obvious attempt to be accommodating and realistic about other religions. It is not mired in an anti-modernism that insists on repeating the doctrines of the past as if the new situation of today is simply to be dismissed. It recognizes the pluralism of the new religious world order as demanding a new and different statement of Christian attitudes towards people of faith outside the church. And yet it attempts this in a way that remains anchored in the core New Testament proclamation of salvation through Christ and no other.

The problem with inclusivism is that—like the exclusivism it tries to get beyond—it remains essentially imperialistic. It offers an interpretation of the mystery of God's grace in other people's lives that is not true to their experience, and that cannot be recognized by them as genuine. A Jew is not likely to be comforted, much less convinced, by the suggestion that she is an anonymous Christian. Nor will a believing Muslim be drawn into the fold of such a redefined Christianity, especially since this is the position already taken by Islam with respect to the church. Islam regards Jesus as a true prophet, but Mohammed as the final prophet. Christianity, in Muslim understanding, is finally to be subsumed under Islam itself. But such positions do not advance mutual respect.

At a World Council of Churches conference in Baar, Switzerland, in 1990, a Roman Catholic bishop from India described the acute difficulties of taking this inclusivist position into actual dialogue with people of other religions. The report of the meeting records the following:

> The bishop recounted his experience of giving a talk in India in which he rather proudly informed his audience that the Catholic church, in Vatican II, had overcome its narrowness and could now proclaim that Hinduism contains "rays of God's truth." Upon which, a Hindu in the audience expressed public gratitude for having been granted at least some "rays" of divine truth. He was matching Hindu irony with Christian condescension.
>
> The bishop admitted his remarks looked like condescension. Some asked whether even such appearances of condescension are compatible with authentic love of neighbour (*Current Dialogue*, January 1991).

Besides the latent but clearly visible imperialism of this position, it suffers from the fatal problem of *reductio ad absurdum*. In other words, it is easily reduced to nonsense because any other religion could logically adopt the same position with respect to Christianity. The Muslim can claim with the same logic that the Christian is simply an "anonymous Muslim" and that Allah has not yet fully revealed his face within the Christian religion; so too can a Jew, a Sikh, and a Buddhist (except that a Buddhist wouldn't). Such intellectual manoeuvres accomplish nothing in the end, and are simply a form of theological sleight of hand, allowing Christians to hold on to their feelings of superiority while giving the impression that they have changed their minds.

The inclusivist position is an attempt to "fit" other religions into our understanding of God, truth, and salvation. It is not an appreciation of them as they are in themselves. It is not an effort at mutual understanding. It fails to recognize the way other faith traditions construct the primary religious questions for themselves and offer their own answers.

The fact is, the religions of the world are not saying the same thing in different ways. One set of ideas cannot be made to fit into another with just a bit of translation. As a Hindu friend once said to me, "What you're offering is not what we're looking for! 'Salvation' does not mean the same as 'enlightenment.'" Non-theistic religions are not doctrinally compatible with theistic ones. The Buddhist concept of nirvana is not the same as the Christian idea of the kingdom of heaven. Nor is the doctrine of the Trinity adaptable to the strict monotheism of the Koran. It is insufficient to say that we will define the content and scope of the world's main religious ideas and then find a way to fit humanity into them. This is not dialogue.

These considerations therefore lead us on to a third position.

Chapter Six

Religious Pluralism

Some Christians, along with many in other traditions, have finally abandoned the idea of the superiority of one religion over all the others. To these believers it seems impossible to continue with the church's historic insistence on its own understanding of God as the only one the world should believe. It appears neither feasible nor desirable to strive for a single belief system for all people. In the words of Rabbi Mattuck, quoted earlier, "I should no more want a world with one religion than I should want only one coloured rose in my garden."

This position takes religious pluralism as more than simply a historical fact, but as the evident will of God for humankind. It is a view arising from the perception that the religions of the world are relatively stable *vis à vis* one another, that they appear in general to be satisfying to their followers, and that there is little objective evidence to demonstrate the preeminence of one over the others. Most "proofs" of superiority tend to come from within each religious system and lack convincing verification from any other standpoint. Pluralism also arises from the deep desire to move beyond both exclusivism and inclusivism, which it regards as unable to break free from the only-one-religion-can-be-true model of reality. It seeks to create a climate of mutual tolerance and respect, an end to religious competitiveness and struggle, to overcome violence and reciprocal suspicion, and to enter into a new humility and openness to others without condescension or paternalism.

It has many forms and champions, but all pluralists agree that there are diverse paths to God, and that God is active among spiritual traditions outside Christianity. All forms of pluralism arise from the belief that religions represent human perceptions of the mystery we call God, that all religious systems are human constructs, and therefore limited and fallible, and that they necessarily reflect the culture, worldview, and thought forms of the people who at different times and places have produced them.

This does not entail the conclusion that religions are therefore false, or simply man-made. It means rather that their truth is established by the grace of God rather than by any definitive proof. It is God who makes religions true. However, we have no reason to suppose that any one religion is truer than the others, because we have no external standpoint from which to judge them all or to weigh their correspondence with the way things actually are. Only God can do that. It seems better, therefore, to suppose that God has revealed himself in a variety of different ways in diverse times and places. If God is present in, and may be known through, a variety of spiritual paths, then they are true paths.

Pluralists see this spiritual variety not as a profusion of error and ignorance, but as a manifestation of the glory of God, as a sign of God's infinite patience in seeking out every nation and people of the world in order to redeem and transform them. It neither surprises nor dismays the pluralist that the resulting perceptions of God have been starkly different and even contradictory. For it is evident that, if God is to be known at all, the divine self-disclosure must be mediated through the culture, language, artistry, and imagination of each of the world's peoples. Each people can only appropriate the knowledge of God in its own way. Each, therefore, will possess a partial perception of all that God may be. But that does not make it false. What is false is the pretension of any one group to possess the whole truth.

It is natural, pluralism argues, that God would wish to be known by people in every nation. It would be absurd for God to create the world and then make the truth known only to one group of people, giving them the task of telling all the others at a time when global communication was physically impossible. Diversity of spiritual understanding is therefore not only inevitable, it is divinely intended. What may appear to us now to be incompatible visions of ultimate Reality are simply our human efforts to see through a glass darkly (1 Cor. 13:12).

Bishop John V. Taylor, in the first Lambeth Inter-faith Lecture given in 1977, comments,

> I think it may often be misleading to speak of the various religions as revelations of God, for that suggests God has disclosed part of himself to one people and a different part to others. Is that how a compassionate Father loves the different children of his family? It is surely truer to believe that God's self-revelation and self-giving is consistent for all, but that different peoples have responded differently (*The Theological Basis of Inter-Faith Dialogue*, 1977).

The foundational paradigm for this way of looking at the world's religions dates back to a now famous parable attributed to the Buddha in the sixth century B.C.E.

> Once there was a certain raja who called to his servant and said, "Come, good fellow, go and gather all the men of Savarthi who were born blind and show them an elephant."
>
> "Very good, Sire," replied the servant, and he did as he was told. He said to the blind men assembled there, "Here is an elephant," and to one man he presented the head of the elephant, to another its ears, to another a tusk, to another the trunk, the foot, the tail, saying to each one that this was the elephant.
>
> When the blind men had felt the elephant, the raja went to each of them and said, "Tell me, what sort of thing is an elephant?"
>
> Thereupon, the man who had been presented with the head answered, "Sire, it is like a pot." The man who had observed the ear replied, "An elephant is like a winnowing basket." The

one who had hold of the tusk said it was a ploughshare. Another said the trunk was a plough; the foot, a pillar; the tail, a brush, and so on.

Then they began to quarrel with each other, shouting loudly, till they came to blows over the matter. The raja was delighted with the scene.

Then the Buddha rendered this meaning: "Just so are the preachers and scholars holding various views blind and unseeing … in their ignorance they are by nature quarrelsome, wrangling, and disputatious, each maintaining reality is thus and so" (*World Scripture: A Comparative Anthology of Sacred Texts*, 1995).

Religious pluralism suggests that, just like the blind disciples grasping parts of a single object, the different religions of the world all grasp hold of God and interpret the divine Reality from their particular perspectives. All are truly connected to God. They are not in fact describing different realities or deities, but their language, images, and symbols are widely disparate. The Buddha regarded theology as the quarrelling of blind men, and concluded that all human knowledge is illusory, including our knowledge of God. But he did not mean by this either that the object of our knowing is false or that the effort to express what we experience in words is necessarily invalid. The story suggests rather that pluralism is inevitable in human systems of thought, and that no system completely describes the ultimate nature of Reality.

The parable is important in two respects. First, it points to the relativity of all knowledge. What human beings can know is always conditioned by their circumstances, their point of access, and their ability to associate what is new with what is already known. Completely detached and objective knowledge of anything is impossible for humans. Second, it is about the elephant. The parable does not suggest that there is no such thing as ultimate truth. It is not a post-modern illustration of the impossibility of knowing anything at all, nor does it suggest that any description of reality is as good as any other. The point is, there is an elephant! The elephant is real.

For modern religious pluralism, this is a vital point. Pluralism is often confused with relativism, the intellectual surrender of hope for any objective knowledge of the real, and the elevation of the self as the ultimate point of reference in human thought and action. Relativism is fashionable in many intellectual circles in the West, and has shaped the individualism and scepticism of our post-religious culture. It is rightly seen as eroding the basis of moral accountability and as replacing religious ideals of responsibility to God and duty to humankind with a disastrous narcissism.

Pluralism is to be distinguished from relativism and also from syncretism. It has not surrendered the concept of truth, nor does it attempt to dissolve conflicting statements about Reality into a single system. Pluralism posits the existence of absolute truth, but argues that all human knowledge of it is conditional and historical. It values the different perceptions of absolute truth, and honours the uniqueness of each spiritual expression. It does not regard the self as the centre of meaning, but urges submission of the individual to the truth as each tradition has received it—in John Hick's phrase, moving from "self-centredness to Reality-centredness." Nevertheless, pluralist theology insists that complete certainty about God or the nature of the "really real" is unattainable for humans or for any of our religions. Therefore, the proper attitude of believers towards one another should be humility, respect, and the abandonment of all claims to absoluteness.

Christian pluralism owes its inspiration to nineteenth-century German liberal theology. One of the key figures in this movement was Ernst Troeltsch (1865–1923). Troeltsch believed religions should be understood historically, that is, as the evolution of human religious ideas. In a lecture given at Oxford University late in his life, he began with the obvious fact that religions change over time:

> Christianity is itself a theoretical abstraction. It presents no historical uniformity, but displays a character different in every age and is, besides, split up into many different denominations, hence it can in no wise be represented as the finally attained unity and explanation of all that has gone before (*The Place of Christianity Among the World Religions*, 1923).

In other words, not only does the Christian religion evolve and change (its character today would be unrecognizable to the apostles and early church leaders), but also it is deeply divided within itself. The multiplicity of denominations within Christianity, each claiming to be the true representative of the faith, fatally undermines the credibility of their claims to absoluteness for all but their own convinced followers. How can all the versions of Christianity be true? How can Christians seriously claim to possess the final revelation of God when they cannot agree among themselves what it is and what its implications are?

Troeltsch argued that religion and culture are inseparable. Religion is one culture's way of expressing its encounter with the living God.

> The great religions might be described as crystallizations of the thought of great races, as these races are themselves crystallizations of the various biological and anthropological forms. There can be no conversion or transformation of one into the other, but only a measure of agreement and of mutual understanding (*The Place of Christianity Among the World Religions*, 1923).

This, incidentally, was also the view of Mahatma Gandhi. Gandhi had great respect for Christianity, and had studied the New Testament when he lived in London. But he strongly disagreed with the activity of Christian missionaries in India, who were attempting to proselytize Hindus. In Gandhi's view, the proper role of a Christian missionary was so to proclaim belief in Christ as to make the Hindu into a better Hindu. Witnessing to one's beliefs is a natural outcome of the passion for truth, Gandhi said, but its correct purpose should be to illuminate rather than to compete. Troeltsch was not so dogmatic, but merely contended that racial identity and religious identity often coalesce together, and that the challenge this presents is not to win one group over to the other but to deepen their mutual understanding.

The obvious question this raises—and it is a question for all pluralist theology—is whether it matters what faith one professes. Is one path as good as another? What reason can a pluralist give for believing in Christ, or for following the Eightfold Path, or for getting up at 5:00 in the morning to begin daily prayer? To this, Troeltsch replied that each authentic faith demands unconditional commitment from its followers, and that this is a necessary devotion for anybody who wishes to know God in any of God's revelations.

> Christianity could not be the religion of a highly developed racial group (such as ours) if it did not possess a mighty spiritual power and truth… It is God's countenance revealed to us; it is the way in which, being what we are, we receive and

react to the revelation of God. It is binding upon us and brings us deliverance. It is final and unconditional for us...

But this does not preclude the possibility that other racial groups, living under entirely different cultural conditions, may experience their contact with the Divine Life in quite a different way, and may themselves also possess a religion which has grown up with them, and from which they cannot sever themselves so long as they remain what they are.

Who will presume to make a final judgement here? Only God himself, who has determined these differences, can do that (*The Place of Christianity Among the World Religions*, 1923).

An important phrase in this response are the words "unconditional *for us*" (emphasis mine). The pluralist position is that the existence of many paths to God does not obviate the obligation within each of them for unconditional and absolute commitment. Rather, it argues that this commitment is absolute only for those who make it, for those to whom it is revealed as an unconditional demand on their lives. This is not the same as claiming a universal absoluteness of one religious system for all people regardless of their own faith decisions. Langdon Gilkey calls this "relative absoluteness."

We must stand somewhere and act from some basis. We need a ground for the apprehension and understanding of reality— a ground that undergirds our choices, our critiques of the status quo, our policies.

We qualify our acknowledged relativism by participating in our quite particular but still stoutly affirmed perspective. Thus ... we uncover a *relative absoluteness* (*Plurality and its Theological Implications*, 1987).

This paradoxical phrase recognizes that, as cultural and historical beings, we have no choice but to commit ourselves to a particular path if we wish to pursue the goal of spiritual understanding. But even as we do that, we must acknowledge the non-absoluteness of the path itself, the necessary limitations of our choice. Such paradox is unavoidable if we wish to leave behind the dangers of religious exclusivism.

If we apply this approach to the famous statement of Jesus in John 14:6, "I am the way, and the truth, and the life. No one comes to the Father except through me," we may perhaps see it in a different light from the exclusivists. Assuming that it is a declaration arising from the Johannine community rather than from Jesus himself (since it appears nowhere else in the gospels), it makes sense to view it as a doxology, an outpouring of praise and unconditional commitment to Jesus as the Messiah. It is a way of saying, Jesus is the only one for us, there can be no other, we are wholly his, and he is truly the incarnation of God.

Marcus Braybrooke comments that this is rather like saying, "Mine is the most beautiful child in the world." On the lips of a happy parent gazing lovingly at a child, this is a perfectly under-standable statement. It would be churlish to treat it as a statement of objective fact and then offer a logical rebuttal. Even the parent understands this. Braybrooke argues that we should treat these abso-lutist statements about Jesus in the New Testament in the same way, as expressions of adoration by those who had experienced new life in him, and as the signs of commitment by his community to an absolute faith in their redemption through him.

It does not deny the truth of Jesus' statement if we see it in terms of its relative absoluteness. Only when the statement is taken out of that context and made into a doctrinal assertion affecting all other spiritual traditions, in effect used as a weapon against other people of faith, does it become untrue. There is no difficulty in the verse if Troeltsch's phrase "for us" is mentally added to it. To the pluralist it then means: Jesus is the way, the truth, and the life *for us* (Christians). None of us comes to the Father except through him. This interpretation preserves the unconditional demand in the statement for those who have chosen Christ as their lord, while allowing for its relative application within the Christian tradition and not to the whole world.

The exclusivist insistence on the literal inerrancy of this passage, and its divine origin, means that inter-faith dialogue becomes impossible for Christians except as a disguise for proselytism. Even as it is, its presence in the New Testament presents many difficulties for people outside the church. Jewish scholar Franz Rosenzweig has commented that "as long as Christianity maintains this statement (John 14:6) as its authentic dogma, there is no place in it for the living God" (*Letters*, 1935).

Perhaps the most influential of modern writers on pluralism has been John Hick. In 1977 Hick called for a "Copernican revolution" in theology; that is, a movement from the view that Christianity is at the centre of the world's religions to the view that God is at the centre, and the various spiritual traditions revolve around the divine. There is, Hick says,

> but one God, who is maker and lord of all; and in his infinite fullness and richness of being he exceeds all our human attempts to grasp him in thought; and the devout in the various great world religions are in fact worshipping that one God, but through different, overlapping concepts or mental images of him (*Whatever Path Men Choose Is Mine*, 1980).

Hick was much impressed by a verse spoken by the Lord Krishna in the Bhagavad Gita, quoted by Swami Vivekananda at the 1893 Parliament of the World's Religions. The verse sums up his pluralistic approach: "However men may approach me, even so do I accept them, for on all sides, whatever path men choose, it is mine" (Bhagavad Gita, 4,11). Following Troeltsch, he argues for the historical relativity of every religion. What determines a person's faith, he points out, is not that one possesses the whole truth and another does not, but simply the accident of birth.

> If someone is born to Muslim parents in Egypt or Pakistan, that person is very likely to be a Muslim; if to Buddhist parents in Sri Lanka or Burma, that person is very likely to be a Buddhist; if to Hindu parents in India, that person is very likely to be a Hindu; if to Christian parents in Europe or the Americas, that person is very likely to be a Christian.
>
> Of course, in each case he may be a fully committed or merely nominal adherent of his religion. But whether one is a Christian, a Muslim, a Jew, a Buddhist, a Sikh, a Hindu—or for that matter a Marxist or a Maoist—depends nearly always on the part of the world in which one happens to have been born.
>
> Any credible religious faith must be able to make sense of this circumstance. And a credible Christian faith must make sense of it by relating it to the universal sovereignty and fatherhood of God.
>
> This is rather conspicuously not done by the older theology, which held that God's saving activity is confined within a single narrow thread of human life, namely that recorded in our own Scriptures (*Christianity and Other Religions*, 1980).

Hick argues that Christianity is not the one and only way of salvation, but one among several, and that Jesus Christ is not the only Saviour. To strengthen and defend this argument he challenges the traditional Christian understanding of the incarnation of God in Christ. He contends that Jesus himself did not claim to be divine. Jesus, rather, pointed his disciples beyond himself to the Father. It was the later church that conceived the idea of his divinity and inserted these claims into the story of Jesus when it was written down.

> Let me first ask the question that is so important to us as Christians, namely, what does all this imply concerning the person of our Lord?... Did he not say "I and the Father are one; no one comes to the Father but by me"?
>
> Whereas until some three or four generations ago it was generally accepted among biblical scholars that Jesus claimed to be the Son of God ... today this is no longer generally held and is indeed very widely thought not to be the case.
>
> The transfer of these titles (Son of God etc.) to Jesus ... has been demonstrated with growing certainty by critical study of the Gospels to be the work of the post-Easter community. Today it must be taken as all but certain that the pre-Easter Jesus neither designated himself as Messiah nor accepted such a confession to him from others.
>
> We cannot rest anything on the assumption that the great christological sayings of the Fourth Gospel (such as "I and the Father are One") were ever spoken, in sober historical fact, by the Jesus who walked the hills and villages of Galilee. It seems altogether more probable that they reflect the developing theology of the Church at about the end of the first century (*Christianity and Other Religions*, 1980).

Here we enter into very disputed realms of New Testament scholarship. While it is true some biblical scholars agree that Jesus never designated himself as the Messiah, it is not true to say that this is a generally held view. The difficulty with all such arguments about "what Jesus actually said" is that they are inevitably speculative. We do not have access to the original tapes. Many scholars, and not only conservative ones, carefully avoid trying to build theories on such historical speculation. We cannot go behind the words in the New Testament. They are all we have. The New Testament now constitutes the record of faith of the church and the words of Jesus in the fourth gospel are firmly part of it.

Wolfhart Pannenberg rejects Hick's argument on this basis. He suggests that the messiahship of Jesus is clearly evident in Jesus' own preaching and teaching. He came to announce the arrival of the kingdom of heaven in himself. The later church merely made clear, when it wrote down the story of Jesus, what he had expressed himself in his call to join him in announcing the forgiveness of sins. This was his radical message, and it was a call to turn away from other options that were available at the time. Otherwise, it would hardly have seemed worth the trouble to the religious authorities of crucifying him (see *Christian Uniqueness Reconsidered*, 1990).

Roman Catholic theologian Hans Küng also attacks Hick's pluralism. It is too simplistic, he says, to claim "all religions are true." Rather, it is more accurate to say that there is truth and error in all religions.

> The boundary between true and false today, even as Christians see it, no longer runs simply *between* Christianity and the other religions, but at least in part *within* each of the religions.
>
> The principle here is that nothing of value in the other religions is to be denied, but neither is anything of no value to be uncritically accepted (*Global Responsibility*, 1991).

This points to the central weakness of the pluralist position. In its attempt at generosity and openness, it fails to establish any norms for judging other religions to be true. It falls prey to its own insistence that there is no standpoint other than God's by which we may claim absoluteness for our own position as Christians. If this is the case, how can we adopt such a standpoint in claiming all religions to be true?

Pluralism appears unable to discriminate between healthy and unhealthy religious beliefs, other than by using criteria drawn from within one or other of the religious traditions. If we want to say that Scientology, for instance, is corrupt and abusive, on what grounds do we do so? For Christians, the principal ground is what we know from the teachings of Jesus. It is by his example that we judge the validity or falsehood of another spiritual message. Yet this is to treat Christian teaching as an absolute from which to view another claim and, according to pluralism, this is unacceptable.

Pluralism seems to entail a suspension of judgement about truth and falsehood within and between the world's religions. There is no way to evaluate their conflicting truth claims. This can lead to a new form of oppression, an absolutism in the sense of an insistence on the equality of everything, in which nothing can be advanced as a definitive claim upon our lives. By treating all religions as equal, pluralists may have abandoned any ground for regarding some doctrines as evil and to be opposed.

Bishop Lesslie Newbigin regards this kind of value-free pluralism as a danger to society.

> The scientific part of our culture continues to flourish because it does not accept pluralism. It does not assume "the parity of all scientific views." Its success depends upon the vigour of the scientific community and upon its willingness to accept the discipline of an established scientific tradition.
>
> In the other half of our culture, that which deals with "beliefs" and "values," this vigour and this discipline are lacking. It would seem that a proposal to sever the search for "salvation" from the business of distinguishing truth from error, is a sign of the approaching death of a culture.
>
> What is certain is that this kind of pluralism will simply crumble in the presence of a confident and vigorous claim to know the truth—such a claim as Islam is at present making with increasing vigour in the contemporary world (*Religion for the Marketplace*, 1990).

Pluralism has difficulty addressing the concern that it does not provide solid enough ground for any spiritual commitment. One way may be as good as another. This does not exactly stir the soul or fire the imagination. It is more likely to lead to spiritual lassitude and indifference. In the context of Western society today, such a position seems more likely to contribute to the erosion of people's spiritual foundations than to shore them up. It encourages people to go their own way rather than directing them forward as an army of resistance to narcissism and global apathy.

Küng's objections to this position are well set forth in his book, *Global Responsibility*. To summarize them briefly:

- there is truth and error in all religions, but this does not mean that they are equally valid
- religions do claim different truths, and they can't all be right
- pluralism is a secular construct; that is, Western, liberal, and modern
- it removes the ground for dialogue by arriving at the conclusion ("all religions are true") before the conversation begins
- it expects of non-Christians what most of them reject—that their own religion is relative and non-absolute
- it expects Christians themselves to deny the uniqueness and finality of Jesus, which is the central criterion of Christian belief.

His concluding observations are helpful in suggesting an alternative both to self-justifying exclusivism and to sentimental pluralism.

If we are to avoid the basic defect of absolutist-exclusivist and relativist-inclusivist positions, a distinction must be made between the view of religions from outside and the view from within.

Seen from outside ... there are of course different true religions. There are different ways of salvation towards the one goal...

Seen from inside, i.e. from the standpoint of believing Christians oriented on the New Testament ... there is only one true religion: Christianity, insofar as it bears witness to the one true God as he has made himself known in Jesus Christ.

However, the one true religion in no way excludes truth in other religions, but can allow their validity.

Insofar as they do not directly contradict the Christian message, other religions can supplement and correct Christian religion and make it more profound.

I said in Chapter 5 at the start of this review of the three possible Christian positions that, in the end, theology by itself will not bring about agreement. This should now be abundantly clear! The threefold classification of Christian attitudes—exclusivism, inclusivism, and pluralism—(first developed by British writer Allan Race) is now increasingly resisted by recent theologians as an incomplete and potentially distorting framework for the contemporary discussion. Thus, Bishop Lesslie Newbigin contends that

> the position I have outlined is exclusivist in the sense that it affirms the unique truth of the revelation in Jesus Christ, but it is not exclusivist in the sense of denying the possibility of the salvation of the non-Christian. It is inclusivist in the sense that it refuses to limit the saving grace of God to the members of the Christian church, but it rejects the inclusivism which regards the non-Christian religions as vehicles of salvation. It is pluralist in the sense of acknowledging the gracious work of God in the lives of all human beings, but it rejects a pluralism which denies the uniqueness and decisiveness of what God has done in Jesus Christ (*The Gospel in a Pluralist Society*, 1989).

This threefold classification is nevertheless helpful in clarifying the profoundly difficult issues that lie at the heart of inter-faith dialogue. It is not good enough, and would surely be rejected by Jesus himself, for Christians to take an imperialistic stance towards the great religious traditions of the world—traditions in which there is an astonishing depth of wisdom and insight into the central mysteries of life and existence under God. But neither is it good enough to adopt an open-ended inclusivity that refuses to address questions of truth, good, and evil, or that surrenders the doctrinal and spiritual ground on which these questions can be answered. This would be to renounce the very role that the spiritual dimension brings to the human situation.

This then raises the further question of whether there might exist some further ground, some non-doctrinal or mystical ground, on which people of faith can meet each other. We shall explore this concept soon, but first let us look at some other important factors that play a role in inter-faith relationships. These have to do with issues of power. For we need to clarify not only the role of theology, prayer, and mystical experience, but also the realities of domination and control.

Chapter 7

The Dynamics of Power

Do people become exclusivists, inclusivists, or pluralists simply for intellectual reasons, by making an abstract theological choice? Is there a "right" theological stance with respect to other religious groups or could each be an appropriate response to certain situations?

In his book *The Dialogical Imperative*, Canadian theologian David Lochhead takes the discussion of theoretical attitudes towards the world's religions into the area of actual concrete relationships. He suggests that real attitudes among people of differing traditions are shaped not so much by theological issues as by the customs, standards, and demands of day to day living through which one community encounters another. It is people's experience, or anticipated experience, that determines their attitude to a cultural or religious stranger.

Lochhead argues that we have to examine the social relationships of religious communities—both within the same religion and among different religious groups—if we are to understand the hidden issues beneath inter-faith dialogue. Relationships, he points out, always involve power. The relative power of one group in relation to another is critical to the theological and spiritual climate that develops between them. He outlines four commonly observed sets of relationships among religious communities. His description of them is illuminating and adds an important dimension to the task of inter-religious understanding.

Isolation

As we noted earlier, the inter-mixing of religious cultures within Western secular societies on the scale we see today is an historically new phenomenon. For most of our history, religious communities have existed in geographic separation from one another. Before global communications allowed people all over the world to see on television the Easter celebrations in St. Peter's Square in Rome, or sacred rituals in the river Ganges, or the swirling crowds around the Ka'ba in the courtyard of the Great Mosque at Mecca, few people heard of these things at all. If they did, it was filtered through the reports of returning explorers or merchants.

In such a closed system of knowledge and experience, the community's own norms and standards are experienced as universal ones. Pluralism is not an option. My neighbour is essentially like me. We are bound by the same rules, and we expect certain beliefs and behaviour to be normative for both of us. Lochhead defines this condition as isolation.

> An isolated community is one in which there is a broad consensus about the way things are. What is true is what everybody knows to be true. Those who contradict what everybody knows to be true are either ignorant, deluded or liars.
>
> The isolated community is not able to take seriously the existence of other views of reality (*The Dialogical Imperative*, 1988).

This cultural and religious insularity can be a strong binding force within a community. It discourages deviation from accepted ethical or social patterns of behaviour and enforces a uniformity of outlook that provides a great cohesive and sustaining power. Such communal societies have survived for centuries all over the world—

among Aboriginal people, for example, before European contact, and in the Americas, Africa, and the South Pacific.

Even people who grew up in rural Canada this century or, as I did, in a tight-knit clannish community in Britain, know the powerful influence of this kind of social formation. Wisdom and knowledge are passed on from generation to generation with the weight of historical certainty. There is an atmosphere of untroubledness in the transmission of ideas. The community's way of life stands on principles that appear self-evident to everyone and need no deep justification. Individuality within accepted parameters is encouraged, but radically new ideas or socially innovative forms of behaviour (especially, in my case, from North America) are treated with suspicion or ridicule.

When people are culturally isolated from one another, they tend to develop exclusive worldviews. Their own traditions and beliefs take shape in a way that cannot take account of other traditions and beliefs. When contact occurs, usually through invasion, migration, or the growth of commerce and trade, there is often a denial of the validity of other ways of thinking and believing, since these call into question the identity and self-understanding of the community which has survived well without them.

This is the form of Christianity we encounter in Europe up until the great colonial and missionary expansion of the sixteenth and seventeenth centuries. Although Orthodox and Oriental Christians had long lived in religiously plural forms of society, Western Christianity until then had no occasion to treat seriously the theological framework of other great belief systems. Only when the wave of imperialist expansion began to wane and collapse in the late nineteenth century did there arise the intellectual climate for self-doubt and openness to new possibilities.

But Lochhead points out that isolation is not simply a matter of geographic separation. People can still be isolated from one another within highly urbanized modern societies. The experience of many people in today's secular society is of isolation from the person next door. There is less likelihood in a contemporary modern city for my neighbour to look like me, or believe as I do, but secularism itself insists that we not try to impose our preferences upon one another. We leave each other alone, and so, paradoxically, envelop each other in another form of spiritual insularity, which leaves us with little opportunity to grow and develop.

Jews in Europe and North America have long lived in the middle of Christian societies, as well as in the Muslim societies of Africa and the Middle East. Though these relationships between minority and majority were sometimes hostile, for the most part they were characterized by mutual isolation. Christians had little to do with Jews, and vice versa. Attitudes of insularity prevailed mutually. So long as contact could be avoided, the equilibrium of life within each community could be more or less sustained. But changing social and economic conditions made this eventually impossible.

As isolation breaks down, Lochhead comments, so does the community's former belief system.

> The view of reality of the community can be successfully challenged only when the community changes, by entering into significant relationships with other communities.
>
> The view of reality is challenged when the community overcomes its isolation (*The Dialogical Imperative*, 1988).

This is precisely what happens in inter-faith dialogue. As people of different faith traditions, each with their unique worldviews and inherited body of wisdom, begin to listen to each other, the former constructions of reality start to shift. Things begin to appear in a new light. Doubts about former certainties start to creep in, and a genuine period of confusion is often precipitated. Those who wish to preserve the former cohesion and stability react in alarm, and tend to strengthen the traditional arguments for exclusivism. From their point of view, they are acting to save the community. Others see the future in terms of new patterns of thinking and new social relationships. It is always a matter of faith and judgement as to which outlook will best serve the needs of the community.

Hostility

When isolation is no longer possible, one of the alternatives is, unfortunately, hostility. Hostility arises when a community feels a threat from another group. Lochhead describes the typical features of this alternative.

Christian history is full of examples in which communities have felt threatened by alternative theologies and have responded by depicting their opponents as enemies of God.

The early theologians described Gnosticism in these terms. Arianism was interpreted in this way by the defenders of Nicaea. Islam, at the time of the Crusades, was understood as a movement against God.

Catholics and Protestants, at the time of the Reformation, felt threatened by each other and described each other in these terms.

Jews, while objectively not much of a threat to the dominant Christian culture in Europe, were perceived as a threat and were described as "Christ killers."

Fundamentalism, a movement born out of the threat of modernity, responded by identifying "modernists" in apocalyptic terms (*The Dialogical Imperative*, 1988).

Mutual isolation is possible only when communities feel little threat from one another. But in a hostile climate, the instincts of self-preservation override all other considerations. The "other" is officially demonized. No longer simply a stranger or an outsider, the other is named as enemy and systematically dehumanized and vilified in the eyes of the community as it prepares itself morally to take violent action in its own self-defence.

Lochhead points out that the threat may be real or imagined. Important in all these different relationships among faith communities is the perceived power of the other group. What people anticipate or expect from each other determines their posture both socially and spiritually. Hostility does not need an overt act to trigger its mechanisms. Lochhead goes on to describe what these mechanisms involve.

The ideology of hostility is distinguished by at least three features. First, the other must be perceived as threatening. Second, the error of the other is not understood as a matter of simple ignorance. The threatening force must be morally culpable. The other is a liar or a deceiver. Third, the other really knows the truth or is the agent of one (i.e. Satan) who knows the truth. The other community is thus perceived as engaged in deliberate warfare against the truth.

This is where religion often plays its most crucial role. Few people are willing to sacrifice their lives or to degrade and kill other human beings for unworthy causes. The innate moral sense in each of us rebels at the thought of casual or unprovoked violence. Not even the incentive of self-interest offered by the promise of commercial opportunities or the lure of fabulous treasure is enough to motivate most people to debase their humanity to the point of assault and murder for no greater cause. The justification has to be deeper, and this is where religion is often co-opted to provide higher moral ground. The Crusades are one such example, but there are many others, and they are found in every religious tradition. The danger of spiritual expropriation by prevailing political interests faces every world religion, and at some time or another every one of them has surrendered to it. We have already described (see Chapter 2) some of the disastrous consequences for human and planetary society of the malevolent corruption of religion.

Yet this is where the self-correcting or self-critical capacity of the more sophisticated traditions can act as a preservative of honesty and truth. In situations where the dominant interests of a community subvert the real message of its religious tradition, there often arises the prophetic voice of protest, a dissenting witness that points people back to the pure and underlying values of the faith, and challenges the community's social and political direction. This was the situation in Germany in the 1930s, for example, when the Confessing Church of German Protestants under the leadership of Karl Barth objected to the co-opting and silencing of the Christian churches by the Nazi regime. The voice of protest can also be found in modern Israel in groups such as the Rabbinic Human Rights Watch, which monitors Israeli treatment of Palestinian prisoners and refugees out of a desire to preserve the moral and prophetic traditions of Judaism in a climate of mutual hostility. In these contexts, the co-opting of religion by demonic or corrupt interests can actually create the conditions for spiritual reform.

Paradoxically, spiritual reform can often take on the characteristics of religious exclusivism. The Barmen Declaration of 1934 by Barth's group of religious dissenters was a product of the extreme conflict between Christian and Nazi ideologies. It was not an inclusivist statement, but a ringing denunciation of social evil and its intellectual foundations in the name of the supreme authority of Christ. Jürgen Moltmann has commented that "the Declaration became the occasion and cause of a need to take a radical stand, and around that rock the waters parted" (*Is Pluralistic Theology Useful?* 1990). Nazi megalomania, and its resulting pervasive and monstrous evil, were thus met by a resolute Christian exclusivism. There could be no compromise between them. And both history and the gospel must judge this to have been an entirely appropriate and necessary response.

It needs to be noted, therefore, that while these first two sets of power relationships—isolation and hostility—tend to produce theologies of exclusion, this may be essential and justifiable in particular circumstances. Their function can often be to preserve and maintain the community of believers against undermining social and spiritual influences, whether real or perceived. They can also act as a corrective against corrupt religion itself, a sort of redemptive resistance movement. In both cases, exclusivism would seem to play a positive role.

Exclusivism, however, can also hold the community back and prevent necessary and desirable social change. This is often the ground on which disputes and conflict arise within religions internally. The current struggles within Western Christianity, for instance, are focused largely on social rather than religious questions. Conflict tends to centre around abortion, homosexuality, and feminism, which then get pushed back into underlying disagreements about biblical interpretation and doctrinal foundations. Outbreaks of internal friction within religions consume great emotional and financial energy, often distracting the faith community as a whole from its primary mission. And yet such conflicts are important precisely to determine the community's attitude to new social conditions and to reshape relationships with other communities.

Competition

The most common relationship among world religions today is still isolation, but second to that, says Lochhead, is competition. This is true especially in pluralistic cultures and societies, where differing religious traditions exist side by side and compete with one another for adherents among the religiously uncommitted. For instance, in the last few years in North America, there has been an impressive (and to some observers startling) growth in Islam, which has begun to make inroads into formerly Christian territory, particularly among urban black youth. This has touched off new tensions between Christianity and Islam, particularly among the conservative elements of each tradition.

Similar tensions are evident in many parts of Africa and Asia where both Christian and Muslim missionary movements vie openly with each other for adherents. In rural communities, churches and mosques try to drown each other out in loudspeaker battles from their roof tops. In some poor countries, one sees a competitive approach to development projects—such as wells, schools, and clinics—as the struggle is waged for the well-being of the people and the advance of the faith. Such struggles can lead to tragic waste and duplication, and can become simply a form of manipulation that exploits poverty and ignorance. It is hard for either side to yield ground to the other, since these local battles become part of a greater one for the supremacy of one religion over its competitor.

The same phenomenon can be noted within the Christian churches themselves, of course. There are two broad streams emerging within modern Christianity, which are locked in a highly competitive relationship with each other. We have seen their increasing divergence over the last forty years. One is the conservative-evangelical-fundamentalist coalition on one side of the theological spectrum, and the other is the modernist-liberal-progressive coalition on the other. Each of them claims to be "orthodox" in belief and practice, but each defines the essence of orthodoxy differently, and each perceives the other as threat and rival. I call them Christian coalitions rather than denominations because these are broadly based theological parties that cut across traditional denominational boundaries. Modernist Anglicans will feel more at home with their Catholic or Presbyterian counterparts than any of them will with conservative opponents within their own church.

Each coalition is developing its own theological position in opposition to the other. Each has created its own theological schools and seminaries, teaching the approved orthodoxies. Each honours its own separate authorities and teachers, and each graduates its own students who have shown a proper understanding of the prevailing notions of truth as well as the egregious errors of their opponents. And each is engaged in a struggle for power within all the mainstream denominations of the church today, attempting to secure senior positions in bureaucracies or to determine legislative policies in central decision-making bodies, in the endeavour to control the church's direction and to deny legitimacy to the perceived adversary.

These relationships are competitive rather than hostile because of the absence of overt violence, but the same conditions of threat are present, and many of the same tactics are employed. Religious competitors tend to portray each other as heretics or false prophets, and themselves as "true" or "orthodox" believers. But competition presupposes a relationship among the parties, a link that binds them together even while they struggle for mutual distinction. David Lochhead describes it this way:

> A competitive relationship has two main characteristics.
>
> In the first place, competing communities implicitly acknowledge that they have some similarities. They are, so to speak, in the same business.
>
> Secondly, competitive communities place considerable stress on their differences. They stress that the ways in which "we" differ from others makes "us" superior.
>
> The competitive attitude is expressed in two ways.
>
> First, it is acknowledged, sometimes grudgingly, sometimes enthusiastically, that other communities are not totally outside the truth.
>
> Secondly, it is insisted, with varying degrees of arrogance, that the full truth is to be found only in the beliefs and practices of our own community (*The Dialogical Imperative*, 1988).

Such a relationship has characterized Protestants and Catholics over the centuries since the Reformation, says Lochhead. They both recognize each other as being in the same "business"—that is, the proclamation of the gospel of Jesus Christ—but they have both emphasized their differences from each other rather than their similarities. Each has laid claim to the truth of the gospel and denounced the heresies of the other. Though there have been times of open hostility and violence between them, and serious efforts to weaken and supplant the influence of the other, the more recent relationship, especially since Vatican II, has been one of competition rather than belligerence. Catholics have given up trying to annihilate Protestants, and vice versa, and now both parties have settled down to the realities of long-term co-existence.

This is characterized by similar efforts in both communities towards nurturing and supporting their own members, teaching the faith as each tradition understands it, providing improved facilities and better services to sustain the mission of the church and attract the unchurched, and evangelizing new Christians by persuasion and example in the effort to build up the body and convert the nations to Christianity. This is a healthy situation from the point of view of history, since the efforts of both communities are now focused on mission and ministry rather than on each other.

Among the great religions of the world, however, the movement from hostility to competition is further behind. This is particularly true where ethnic and racial divisions correspond to religious ones. In parts of Africa, for example, Islam presents itself as the religion of Africans and appeals to racial identity as part of its call to follow the teachings of Mohammed. Christianity is frequently depicted as a foreign religion, as the religion of Europe, the whites, the oppressors. African Christians respond with indignation and denial. Churches are burned and mosques are destroyed in a self-perpetuating pattern of religious civil war that divides communities and families, and creates lasting animosities. In such situations, the growth of a spirit of mutual competition would be an improvement on the present climate.

Competitiveness in religion implies the granting of a measure of truth to each other by the parties. There is a recognition that what each is offering is a distinct perspective on a commonly accepted Reality, or more exactly, a more comprehensive and accurate account of that Reality and its claim upon our lives. Fundamental disagreements about the nature of religious truth or its implications can often obscure the deeper underlying unity that binds the different parties together in a shared enterprise and common goal. When such commonalities are recognized and acknowledged, the possibility of partnership and mutuality begins to appear. But the essence of competitive relationships is that people are more disposed to see differences than similarities, and any attempt at mutual dialogue is regarded as betrayal of the principles for which the separate parties stand.

Paradoxically, it is in Western, secularized, pluralistic societies that competition—as distinct from hostility—among the world's religions has become possible. Western secularism is intolerant of quests for religious supremacy and indifferent to the question of which religion has more truth than others. Most modern people are suspicious of religion's potential to divide and aggravate our increasingly diverse societies, and are conscious of the disastrous history of religious wars in the West. Thus in most industrial societies there is, by general consensus, a deliberate neutrality imposed on all religious combatants with respect to public policy and public institutions (such as schools), and an attitude of mutual tolerance required from them towards each other. This forces the different faith communities to compete with each other without the threat of violence. Each must commend the truth it proclaims on the basis of conviction not coercion, holiness not violence. Secularism, which is much attacked by religious traditions of every kind, has in some measure achieved what the religions themselves could not—an end to the social threat of religious aggression.

The movement from hostility to competition can therefore bring the different faith communities into a healthier relationship with each other, at least in the sense that it forces them to present their best face towards the world rather than their worst. Secularism, precisely because of its indifference to religious matters, has created not only a healthy competitive spirit among religions but also strong competition to religion itself. The values of religious faith have been widely replaced by those of consumerism and individualism. In modern societies, among every faith tradition, religious observance is in serious and even catastrophic decline. Religions can no longer afford to presume that their mutual struggles for supremacy have any meaning for the vast majority of people. The task now is to win converts.

This is where the missionary religions, especially Christianity and Islam, tend to thrive. The positive aspects of each of these faith traditions are now being presented to the uncommitted public in order to show the beneficial effects of the spiritual paths they represent. Much emphasis is being placed on education and formation in the spiritual disciplines. Much attention is being given to community outreach and support for the needy. Christianity is seeking to reclaim its place within the Western world by a process both of modernization and historical re-affirmation. Islam presents itself as a radical alternative both to consumerism without purpose and spirituality without structure. While these efforts may or may not be successful in turning back the tide of religious decline, they nevertheless provide a momentum for renewal of the religions themselves.

Partnership

The fourth type of relationship that can exist among faith communities is that of partnership. This possibility emerges when people begin to focus primarily on what unites them rather than on what divides, when they come to see the similarities as more significant than the differences. It occurs when a sense of kinship or common ground starts to replace the sense of rivalry and competition, and the distinct faith communities begin to look at what elements of faith or mission they can share rather than what advantage they can take of one another.

Lochhead points to his own church, the United Church of Canada, as an example of this. It was formed as a result of growing ecumenical sentiment among Canadian Christians belonging to the Congregational, Methodist, and many Presbyterian churches. It was a response to the challenge of the vast and expanding mission field of Canada in the 1920s, especially the settlement of the Prairies and the West, which seemed to defy the pettiness of traditional relationships and called for a spirit of mutuality and friendship to tackle a project larger than any of the churches was capable of doing alone. The United Church is to this day deeply committed to ecumenism and partnership with other Christian churches and faith groups, and has recently begun to redefine ecumenism to include the world religions, indeed, the whole created order (see *Toward a Renewed Understanding of Ecumenism*, United Church of Canada, 1994).

The churches of Canada, in fact, offer a model of partnership unique in the world. For over twenty-five years now, all the major mainstream denominations have participated in coalitions for social justice, that have brought together Christians of many backgrounds in a common task of witness and advocacy for social change. Perhaps because of the distances across the nation and the small population, or perhaps because Canada has never been a colonial power like some European countries, there has developed here a tradition of partnership, which is found in the culture and in the churches themselves. As a result, we have evolved common approaches to many public policy questions, including Aboriginal rights, immigration, poverty, environmental protection, human rights, and overseas development assistance.

Among Christian churches, partnership has become possible most easily around the issues of justice and society. Christians of differing traditions can agree more readily on the concrete application of faith than upon their doctrinal sources of authority. While many remain theologically divided—for example, unable to receive communion together at ecumenical celebrations of the Eucharist—they can nevertheless be politically united in the face of an agreed social evil or threat to human well-being. This suggests partnership can exist on many levels. Theological and doctrinal agreement is not necessary for religious believers to work together.

Not surprisingly, therefore, a great deal of inter-faith activity exists at the level of common social action. In Britain, the growth of inner-city poverty among immigrant groups, and the danger of racial intolerance and community violence, have brought together associations of Christians, Jews, Muslims, Baha'is, Hindus, and Sikhs in a mutual quest for solutions. In the United States, a broad coalition of opposition to the rising power of the religious right-wing has united Jews and Christians of the political centre and left to defend civil and religious liberties in the face of legislative assault. In Canada, churches work with partner agencies in the developing world, some of them secular and some of other faith traditions, to attack hunger and under-development among the world's poorest peoples. In the Middle East, Muslims, Jews, and Christians take great risks to witness together for peace between Arabs and Israelis, and hold inter-faith services of prayer to try to calm community fears.

Most inter-faith work is aimed at generating new levels of cooperation and understanding among divided peoples rather than resolving doctrinal and theological differences. This is the focus of much of the work initiated around the world since the 1893 Parliament of the World's Religions. But at the same time, there have been gatherings of scholars and teachers, mystics and monks, of various traditions to work on the task of finding common ground within the difficult areas of creed and dogma. There is an attempt to discover and build a theology of partnership that discerns the similarities and kinship among religions, the unitive principles, in order to open up the possibility of global unity among believers. This is the work to which an increasing number of theologians of all traditions are now committed. And though they are often divided on the best approach to the question, nonetheless this represents one of the most important frontiers of modern thought.

For those of us who have moved beyond hostility and competition to a sense of partnership with other believers, there has also been a compulsion to move from a theology of exclusivism to theologies of inclusivism or pluralism as well. I state it this way quite deliberately. In my experience, people do not argue themselves intellectually into new relationships with strangers. It seems rather to be the other way round. We act ourselves into new ways of thinking.

The new context of modern society, particularly secular society with its positive tolerance of diversity and its negative indifference to faith, has brought many of us to a sense of the inadequacy of established theological postures. Some of us are searching for new theologies altogether. Others are searching traditional sources of faith for new ways forward based on known ways of old. Along this journey we are inevitably influenced by the nature of our encounter with people of other religions. Those we experience as threat and danger we attempt to exclude and reject. Those we experience as neighbour and friend force us to rethink our inherited assumptions and to enlarge our understanding. Christian theology is not created in a vacuum. It is the reflected experience of the believing community. In this sense it is often reactive.

Yet the teaching of the church has tremendous formative power too. It shapes our attitudes and behaviour towards the stranger and the alien. We can search the face of the newcomer to find Christ there (inclusivism), or welcome her as a fellow pilgrim in the company of God (pluralism), or regard his arrival as an opportunity to enlarge the church (exclusivism). Whatever the choice, our relationships will be determined for better or worse.

Chapter 8

The Mystical Path

*H*ans Küng has classified the historic world religions into three types:

PROPHETIC	MYSTICAL	WISDOM
Judaism	*Buddhism*	*Confucianism*
Islam	*Hinduism*	*Taoism*
Christianity		

The *prophetic* religions are those whose primary orientation is towards this world and its transformation under God. Though each of the three traditions of this type varies considerably from one another, their common characteristic is a commitment to revealed truth. For Christians, of course, this is Christ. For Muslims, the Koran. For Jews, it is the tradition of law beginning with Moses. Each faith community has its own authoritative scriptures. These writings, along with their respective histories of oral interpretation, are normative for their followers, form the basis of instruction for new converts, and guide the development of ethical teaching and political action.

The *mystical* religions have a largely other-worldly orientation. Their concern is to penetrate beyond the surface appearance of things and to discern the ultimate Reality uniting all existence. Physical reality is only partly real, never ultimate. Human existence is not limited to one lifetime. Again, the religions of this type differ from one another in important respects, but their common characteristic is a commitment to unity and harmony in a cosmic sense. For the Buddhist, the goal of existence is nirvana, the final absorption of the self into the pleroma beyond birth and death. For the Hindu, the goal varies among the many traditions, but is generally to escape from the material world into ultimate unity with the divine. These traditions have no single scriptural authority or corporate liturgical rituals such as Christian weekly worship or Muslim daily prayer. They manifest themselves in personal devotion, at-home shrines and public monuments, as well as in community festivals.

The *wisdom* religions seek enlightenment as the goal of human existence. They are both worldly and other-worldly in orientation, since enlightenment consists in a balance of both knowing and not-knowing. Their characteristic is a striving towards perfect human acceptance of the metaphysical order, which is to be found by entering into progressive stages of deeper understanding, set out in clearly defined spiritual paths. The authoritative guides are not written scriptures but personal mentors, gurus, and teachers, those who have gone ahead along the path and know the way. Every facet of life in these traditions has a ritual aspect. Sacred and secular are indistinguishable to the enlightened mind.

Küng defines a religion as a global "paradigm," that is, a total constellation of meaning, a worldview encompassing everything. Religions manifest themselves in unique symbols, language, doctrine, and outlook. No religion offers a partial understanding of reality. A religion, by definition, constitutes its own paradigm, its own total constellation of meaning. It offers a way of understanding everything in the cosmos, from personal life to global destiny, and therefore offers a model of living for every particular circumstance. There is literally nothing outside the scope of a religion.

For this reason, different religions cannot be reduced to a single system. It would not be possible to harmonize the prophetic, mystical, and wisdom religions into one paradigm that would successfully incorporate the elements of each. Any attempt to do so would produce either a tossed salad of separately extracted pieces thrown together in a mixing bowl, or else a whipped purée—a reduced, boiled-down strain of all the religions blended together in something quite unrecognizable to anyone. For the same reason, it is difficult to translate elements of one paradigm into another. Because of the sophisticated character of religious symbols and their stated and hidden meanings, and the complex inter-relationship of ideas, rituals, and language within each religious system, it is unwise and ultimately unproductive to try to apply the concepts and doctrines of one system to those of another. An example of this came my way some years ago.

As a clergyman I rarely sit in a pew. One Sunday, though, I had the weekend off and went to a nearby church with some members of my family for a baptism. The church was conservative evangelical, and the preacher that morning was a young woman who had just returned from a trip to Asia on behalf of an organization for global evangelism. In her sermon she described the religions of the countries she had visited. She told us how she went to one shrine where she found no one worshipping. There was a bell at the entrance. Her guide informed her the bell was to wake up the god inside. She proceeded then to ridicule a religion whose gods went to sleep, and where no one went to pray, and compared them with the God of Jesus Christ who is eternally present with us and knows the hairs of our head. She invited us to join her in evangelizing those who have no knowledge of salvation.

The sermon distressed me because it displayed a deep ignorance of the symbolism and practices of other spiritual traditions and treated them with contempt. The preacher had encountered something new and foreign to her experience—a religion, unlike Christianity, with no tradition of public liturgy or corporate celebration. In Asia, public shrines and monuments usually have more of a cultural than a religious significance, because Hindus, Buddhists, Confucians, and followers of the Tao believe it is not necessary to go to a place of worship to show devotion to God.

What she had witnessed, in all likelihood, was a Hindu *puja* ritual in which, every morning, the statue or picture of a god is "wakened" with *puja* sounds such as bells, light, food, perfume, and prayers. It is a morning ritual, often performed by families together as a kind of daily office. Hindu gods are regarded as intermediary beings, more than human but less than the ultimate God or Brahman. Without understanding, it is easy for Christians to denounce what they see as idolatry and paganism, but we should remember that Christians perform their own strange rituals with bells, perfume, lights, and food, which can appear nonsensical to an outsider. We need to be careful about forming judgements from external appearances.

The sermon also guilelessly assumed that these unevangelized souls were waiting to hear the good news about "salvation." Küng's observations are important here. "Salvation" is a concept whose meaning resides within the Judeo-Christian tradition. It is part of a complex system of language and ideas that has developed within our particular history, and it has no meaning apart from that. In order to offer the knowledge of salvation to someone, one needs to offer them the whole system of Christian belief and practice. One needs to change their paradigm, their worldview, language, symbolism, their total meaning system—to replace their mental universe with another. This, of course, is what the preacher had in mind, but without an understanding of the different religious systems, her efforts were likely to be unproductive or even damaging.

Salvation is not something a Buddhist or a Hindu desires. Even if the concept could be sufficiently explained across the paradigm gap, or winningly presented by examples of Christian holiness, the ultimate goal of faith for the mystical or wisdom believer is something else. Just as for the Christian or the Jew "enlightenment" in the Eastern sense is not part of our consciousness or vocabulary, and efforts to evangelize us towards this end would require a considerable degree of translation to be intelligible, so too with the proclamation of the gospel to members of other religions. We cannot assume that what we have to offer is something other believers actually want.

Küng's classification of the three types of religion therefore warns us against the simple transposing of religious words from one system to another. Salvation is not another word for enlightenment. Nirvana is not the same as heaven. How each faith community conceives the central project of human existence, the purpose and goal of the spiritual life, is not only expressed in different words, but may also have quite distinctive end-points in view.

This does not mean that inter-faith understanding is from the outset impossible. The point of these distinctions is principally to underline the need for dialogue, and to illuminate the unavoidable requirement of listening deeply in order to hear what others are saying. Inter-faith dialogue is not simply the business of translating their words into ours and declaring some falsely constructed ground on which to presume agreement. Nor can we suppose our own sacred ideals to be self-evidently universal in appeal. Inter-faith dialogue is like entering into another person's thought-world, seeing Reality through different eyes, enlarging each one's understanding of truth.

There is an analogy here with learning a foreign language. I am an English-speaking person, for example. In order to learn German, I must study its vocabulary, learn a different sentence structure, acquire a grasp of its grammar. The best way to do this is to engage myself in conversation with German-speaking people. In time I may be able to speak the language fluently, but as I do that, I am gradually drawn beyond the language itself. As I come into relationship with German-speaking people, I begin to discern a different culture, something that gives both the language and the people a common identity. It's a different way of doing things, of seeing things. Learning German is not simply a matter of learning the words, but of entering into a distinctive culture.

In the same way, many people have made the journey into other religious cultures. They have become bilingual in the spiritual sense. From their explorations and experiences have come reports of a common essence among religions, a fundamental unity beyond doctrines and dogmas. They will often observe that there is no possibility of finding *theological* harmony among the spiritual traditions, for no way exists to reconcile teachings that are irreconcilable, but that at some deeper level all religions are one. This idea has an obvious appeal to anyone interested in inter-faith dialogue.

A Common Essence?

Could it be that the differences among religions are merely external? Is it possible that at the core of each religion lies the same Reality, the same God, however differently named? It is a common enough assumption today, even among people who have no faith commitment, that different religions are simply different expressions of belief in the one God.

Appealing as this is, there is an immediate difficulty with it. Not all religions profess belief in God or in a god. The non-theistic religions, such as Buddhism and the Advaita Vedanta school of Hinduism, hold no such belief. Are we to say therefore that these are not religions in the true sense? This argument is sometimes made, but it seems to be an effort more to preserve a definition (religion equals belief in God) than to facilitate inter-faith understanding. Certainly, it would be impossible to exclude Buddhists from the study of religions. They bring enormous insights to the question of what may lie beyond the external appearances of religion.

Many theologians of the pluralist school today prefer not to use the word *God* at all. They often speak of the Ultimate, or the Real, or the Transcendent, to designate that final end towards which religious faith draws us on. It is a characteristic of religions to have a basic orientation towards transcendent reality, the Really Real, which stands over and above us, beneath and within human experience. Some of them name this transcendent reality in personal terms—Father, Lord, Jahweh, Allah, Parmeshwar, Ahura Mazda, Satchidanand, and so on—and others in non-personal terms. This fundamental issue of whether God is personal or not, a being, Being-itself, or even non-Being, poses great difficulty in inter-faith conversations.

Yet even this basic difference may be part of the external nature of religion. Neither the personal nor impersonal descriptions of the Transcendent may be entirely accurate. Is it possible that there is a "God beyond God," as Paul Tillich maintained, One who stands completely outside our human ability to comprehend, yet who is revealed in all religions? Is it possible that this same Reality is known in both personal and non-personal terms alike?

Of all the historic religions, Hinduism is the most comfortable with this idea. Let us recall Swami Vivekananda's words at the 1893 Parliament of the World's Religions in Chicago.

> Do not care for doctrines, do not care for dogmas or sects or churches or temples; they count for little compared with the essence of existence in each man which is spirituality.
>
> All religions, from the lowest fetishism to the highest abso-lutism, are so many attempts of the human soul to grasp and

realize the Infinite, as determined by the condition of birth and association.

In the Bhagavad Gita, the Lord Krishna says: "I am in every religion as the thread through a string of pearls."

Every religion is only an evolving of God out of material man. The same God is the Inspirer of all (*Pilgrimage of Hope*, 1992).

The appeal to unity here is at the level of mystical experience. In the Hindu view, there cannot be any logical or theoretical reconciliation of religious teachings, but there is a common spiritual experience. There is the possibility of the same mystical enlightenment for any serious disciple who penetrates deeply enough into the spiritual path he or she has chosen. In order to do this, one has to go beyond the externals of each religion and enter into its depth. There, it is said, the differences dissolve and communion becomes possible.

Buddhism would affirm this belief as well. The Buddha taught that "logic, inference, and reasoning" are obstacles to enlightenment. He warned that scepticism was one of the fetters from which the true disciple must be freed. In order to achieve enlightenment, the intellect must be removed from the picture. In one of his most famous parables he makes the point quite graphically.

The monk Malunkyaputta, upset by the fact that the Enlightened One would preach at the same time "the world is eternal and the world is not eternal, the world is finite and it is infinite, the soul and body are identical and they are not identical, the after life neither exists nor does not exist ..." asked him to explain this puzzle. He obtained the following answer:

"It is as if a man had been wounded by a poisonous arrow and, while his family and friends would hasten to find him a doctor, this man would say, 'I will not have the arrow removed before I know if the one who wounded me is a warrior, a brahman, his name, and to what clan he belongs, whether he is tall or short, black, brown or yellow."

The Enlightened One proclaimed himself free from any theory, its thesis or antithesis. Asking for a resolution of the irreconcilable is like asking "When a flame goes out, which way does it go—north, south, east or west?" (Mircea Eliade, *World Religions*, 1991).

How ridiculous, says the Buddha, if you have been struck by an arrow to ask after the kind of person who fired it. What you need is a doctor! In the same way, asking after the true nature of God or the Transcendent is to pursue the wrong question. It is like asking where a flame goes when it goes out. These rational blindfolds need to be abandoned. You can know God despite God's unknowability. Put aside the demands of reason and learn to believe. Do what is important for your eternal health, not what is unnecessary and irresolvable.

The message here is common to many wisdom traditions, including those familiar to Christians, Jews, and Muslims. It is necessary to *believe* in order to understand. True understanding is a consequence of right orientation to Reality, not the other way round. The vehicle of this message, particularly in the Buddha's teaching but also in the parables of Jesus, is *paradox*. Paradox is the main tool of the mystic. It deliberately confounds logic. It appeals to wisdom's sense of ambiguity, to truth's inner simplicity. The power of paradox lies not in its rational persuasiveness but in its spiritual illumination.

Mystics and Monks

It is the mystics, rather than the theologians, who have explored most deeply the contours of religious experience. Each tradition has produced its spiritual masters, its learned sages whose life of prayer and meditation has deeply enriched the faith community, and sometimes the world.

In every religion, spiritual experience is expressed through the language and rituals of that tradition, but there appears to be a universality of religious experience. It is suggested by similar forms of ecstatic prayer, monastic discipline, self-denial, meditation, and even silence. Across many religious traditions one can observe people engaged in similar rituals and practices, and read similar accounts of people experiencing the divine through visions, trances, spiritual exercises, and prayer. It is plausible to suppose that religious experience has similar characteristics whatever the religion of the adherent. And this leads to the inference that genuine spiritual experience flows from communion with the same God or transcendent Reality. At least this is a possibility, and it has attracted much interest among mystics and monks over the years across a number of traditions. Some of them have been Christians.

Meister Eckhart (1260–1320) is an early example. He was a German Dominican monk, and both a mystic and a logician. His poems and writings all concentrate on God as the starting point of mystical experience. Eckhart was struck by the fact that God is. The existence of God was for him a fascinating fact. In the deep contemplation of God, he taught, we can come into the very presence of the divine. He called this presence by many names: the Wordless Godhead, the Naked Godhead, the Nameless Nothing, the Still Wilderness, the Immovable Rest. Like the Buddha, he explored the similarities and dissimilarities between divine and human wisdom. He used paradox to remove false obstacles to spiritual experience.

Asceticism is of no great importance.

There is a better way to treat one's passions than to pile on oneself ascetic practices which so often reveal a great ego and create more, instead of less, self-consciousness.

If you wish to discipline the flesh and make it a thousand times more subject, then place on it the bridle of love. Whoever has accepted this sweet burden of the bridle of love will attain more and come much further than all the penitential practices and mortifications that all the people in the world acting together could ever carry out.

Whoever has found this way needs no other.

It is when people are not aware of God's presence everywhere that they must seek God by special methods and special practices. Such people have not attained God.

To all outward appearances, people who continue properly in their pious practices are holy. Inwardly, however, they are asses. For they know about God, but do not know God (Matthew Fox, *Meditations with Meister Eckhart*, 1982).

There is a striking similarity between this last statement of Eckhart and a passage in the Tao TeChing: "Those who say do not know. Those who know do not say."

Here we find the appeal to *love* as the ground of mystical knowledge and communion with God. Love is the realm in which the divine and human meet. Love is the basis of genuine religious experience, and those who engage in the outward manifestation of rituals without the inner quality of devotion and adoration are simply "sounding gongs or clanging cymbals" (1 Cor. 13:1).

In a remarkable parallel with Buddhism, Eckhart taught the paradox of dying to self in order to find self. It was based, of course, on Jesus' teaching in Matthew's gospel—"those who find their life will lose it, and those who lose their life for my sake will find it" (10:39). But Eckhart takes this beyond physical self-denial, and even total commitment to Christ, and suggests an almost nirvana-like absorption of the soul into non-Being:

> For the will to be free, it needs to let go and return to its prime origin.
>
> For the intellect to be free, it must become naked and empty and by letting go return to its prime origin.
>
> Think of the soul as a vortex or whirlpool and you will understand how we are to sink eternally from negation to negation into the One, and how we are to sink eternally from letting go to letting go into God (*Meditations with Meister Eckhart*, 1982).

Eckhart's spiritual method is called the via negativa, the way of negation. It was a much used technique among medieval Christian mystics. Its purpose is to negate what is known in order to prepare the mind and heart for the unknown mystery of God. The images and pictures of the divine we have in our conscious minds need to be cleared away. They become obstacles preventing the dramatic reality of God from taking possession of us. The intellect has to be cleansed and purified of all that is not-God in order for us to draw near to the true God. Thus one of Eckhart's most startling statements: "I pray God to rid me of God. The highest and loftiest thing is to let go of God for the sake of God. God's exit is His entrance."

For many Christians, especially those of us who live in consumer-oriented societies that encourage gratification and pleasure, this negating approach to spiritual practice is foreign and perplexing. It represents the very opposite of the charismatic experience, for instance, which places such emphasis on joyful spirit-filled sensation. And yet Eckhart's description of self-emptying and of self-annihilating absorption into the divine is instantly recognizable to people of faith around the world, and to Christians with experience in traditional spiritual exercises, as an authentic path to spiritual knowledge. It offers, perhaps, one of the mystical bridges across which people of faith can pass and connect with each other through common experience. By negating our limited images of God and allowing the soul to be repossessed by divine love, we transcend theology and dogma for the sake of a higher communion with each other and with the Nameless Nothing, which is at the heart of everything.

Another contributor to this mystical bridge-building is Mechtild of Magdeburg (1210–1280). She was a contemporary of Eckhart in the German mystical school, and a Beguine nun. The Beguines were not an order, but communities of women living and praying together. Their aims were philanthropic; they served the sick and the poor, and they developed the practice of spiritual contemplation. They ran afoul of the ecclesiastical authorities, who suspected them of heresy, and endured a century of persecution.

The grounds of suspicion were laid by women such as Mechtild herself, who was a visionary and mystic and, though well versed in Scripture, allowed her imagination to soar well beyond the images and ideas with which church leaders were familiar. She saw the fundamental unity of all things enfolded in the mystery of God: "The day of my spiritual awakening was the day I saw, and knew I saw, all things in God and God in all things" (Sue Woodruff, *Meditations with Mechtild of Magdeburg*, 1982).

One of the characteristics of mysticism in all religious traditions is a vision of harmony at the centre of creation. This harmony is distorted but not destroyed by existential differences. The seer, the one who cultivates deep spiritual insight, can always discern the unity that both holds together and transcends all human differentiation. Hinduism and Buddhism (the mystical religions), for example, have a deep commitment to the profound oneness of things. For this reason, mysticism tends to discount the importance of differences, to blur distinctions or simply not to notice them at all.

The Western religious traditions, on the other hand, tend to concentrate on distinctions as a way to clarify truth. Prophetic religion is inclined to place greater value on right belief than on unity. It tends to overlook the possibility of harmony within and beyond external separation. The focus is often on intellectual precision about doctrinal statements, which can and does lead to religious conflict.

However, there are teachings in the mystical schools of all the historic Western traditions to counteract this. They emphasize the importance of surrendering the will, detaching the intellect, renouncing passions and desires, absorption into the holy, and adoration of the sacred. Their primary concern is not for theological precision but for union with the divine. Mechtild is representative of these techniques. She refused to separate the human and the divine in the traditional dualistic way. She saw a deep interpenetration of the two, so that humanity itself contains the essential elements of the Spirit of God.

> God has so enfolded the soul into Himself, and so poured out the divine nature so completely into it, that the soul is rendered speechless. It says nothing except that God is in the closest communion with it, and God is more than a Father.
>
> God says: "Do not fear your death. For when that moment arrives I will draw my breath and your soul will come to Me like a needle to a magnet" (*Meditations with Mechtild of Magdeburg*, 1982).

These are images rather than concepts. They invite us towards an attitude of wonder and devotion, rather than demanding rational or cognitive assent. And yet they point to a consciousness that one finds in mystics worldwide. In the Hebrew Scriptures we find images of life and death expressed in terms of the breathing out and the breathing in of God. The human spirit or soul is the indwelling breath—ruah—of Jahweh. When God breathes out, life begins. When God breathes in, matter returns to dust and life departs. Life and death, therefore, in the Hebrew mystical tradition, is nothing less than the breathing out and breathing in of God. This is their beauty and their simplicity. Here is the basis of Ezekiel's vision of the valley of the dry bones (Ezek. 37) coming to life as the wind of God passes over it until finally a nation rises.

We can find this consciousness also in the Upanishads, the sacred writings of the Vedanta philosophy of Hinduism. These spiritual treatises describe the relationship of the soul to the universe in Hindu thought. God, or Brahman, is central to all existence—both immanent and transcendent, within and beyond. What appear on the surface to be separate orders of being, distinctive realities like animals, humans, trees, mountains, flowers, and so on, are in fact illusory. They are different expressions of the one reality, which is Brahman.

This is the truth. As sparks fly from a blazing fire by the thousand, so also my good friend do various beings come forth from the imperishable God and return to him again.

He is self-illuminating and formless, uncreated and existing both within and without. He is devoid of mind and pure. Of him are born mind and body, air, fire, water and earth, which supports all.

In truth, God alone is the universe, which consists of work and austerity. O my good friend, he who knows this God, the supreme and the immortal, hidden in the cave of the heart, cuts asunder even here the knot of ignorance *(Mundaka Upanishad, II. 1. 10).*

The parallels between these ancient writings and the poems of European ascetics centuries later are all the more striking because they could have had no contact with each other whatsoever. We have much more access today to the sacred writings of the world's religions than anyone in the thirteenth century. These writings display common threads and themes, which suggest a set of common spiritual experiences reached quite independently of one another. Such congruity leads to the supposition that, despite external differences of expression, the great religions of the world are connected to the same divine truth.

Suspecting this, a more recent Christian mystic who set out to explore the spiritual riches of the East was Thomas Merton (1915–1968). He is perhaps better known to us than these distant figures from the thirteenth century. A Trappist monk in Kentucky, U.S.A, he was also a poet, writer, political commentator, social activist, and silent contemplative. His extraordinary mind ranged over a wide variety of subjects from the Rule of Benedict to Zen painting, from the Vietnam War to marijuana smoking. A liberal Catholic, he was a savage critic of secularism and capitalism, and deplored the identification of Christianity with Western politics and consumerism. It was the spirit of Vatican II that inspired Merton to explore the mystical practices of the Eastern monastic traditions, especially Buddhism.

Merton addressed the Temple of Understanding conference in Calcutta in 1968, organized by Juliet Hollister and her friend Eleanor Roosevelt (see Chapter 3). In his opening remarks, he made an observation about the intimate relationship between Christianity and

Buddhism he had discovered on his trip to Asia: "We are already one, but we imagine that we are not. What we have to recover is our original unity. What we have to be is what we already are" (*The Asian Journal of Thomas Merton,* 1973).

The comment is based on a remark of St. Augustine, yet Merton took Augustine's understanding of "original unity" out of its philosophical home and gave it a new global and ecumenical dimension. On his 1968 trip, he visited the Theravada Buddhists in Sri Lanka, Hindus and Christians in India, and had three interviews with the Dalai Lama in Dharamsala. These experiences were life-changing. In these interviews he discussed Eastern and Western forms of monasticism, noted with astonishment the advances of the Buddhists in active contemplation, and allowed himself to enter into the world of Asian ascetic disciplines.

His diary of these experiences, later published as *The Asian Journal of Thomas Merton,* is a fascinating collection of jottings and notations revealing an insatiable curiosity. They show a deep respect for the insights of Eastern culture. Though often critical, they are always an effort to get inside the Eastern mind and to try to experience things from a non-Western point of view. Merton's openness and sympathy towards new religious experience led him to confirm for himself the importance of crossing boundaries and taking the risk of discovering God in other places.

> In all the great world religions there are a few individuals and communities who dedicate themselves in a special way to living out the full consequences and implications of what they believe.
> Those forms of special contemplative dedication include:
> a) a certain distance or detachment from the ordinary and secu-lar concerns of worldly life;
> b) a preoccupation with the radical inner depth of one's religious or philosophical beliefs;
> c) an eventual breakthrough and discovery of a transcendent dimension of life beyond that of the ordinary self, and of ethical and pious observance (*Asian Journal,* 1973).

Merton was a voracious reader of Eastern writers and an avid conversationalist with gurus and Zen masters. The spiritual disciplines of the Buddhist monastic tradition appealed to him. The idea of stages in spiritual progress, the notion of paradox, the final necessity of the leap of faith—these were very stimulating in his search to deepen his own understanding. The notion of freedom lying at the heart of discipline, of an essence indwelling all externals, had a profound ring of truth to him. And yet his intellectual freedom arose from his firm rootedness in the Christian tradition. For Merton, intellectual freedom is one of the gifts of the Christian life, and he regarded his exercise of it not as rebellion but as faithfulness. From his secure base as a Catholic, he could wander far afield without fear of losing his way.

> We have now reached a stage (long overdue) of religious maturity at which it may be possible for someone to remain perfectly faithful to a Christian and Western monastic commitment, and yet to learn in depth from, say, a Buddhist discipline and experience.
>
> I believe that some of us need to do this in order to improve the quality of our own monastic life and even to help in the task of monastic renewal which has been undertaken within the Western church (*Asian Journal*, 1973).

What Merton learned from the East was a quality of seeing, of seeing-through and within. His gurus and guides taught him to look beyond the particular and to notice the universal. They stressed that knowing is not the same as knowing about. In an entry in the Journal, he describes one of his visits to the Dalai Lama. On the first occasion, he had been taken up a hillside to the residence, past ramshackle dwellings and odd people. On the second occasion, making the same journey, he saw the same people and the same things in a totally new way.

> The "mandala" awareness of space.
>
> For instance, this mountain, where a provisional Tibetan pattern of dwellings and relationships has been, very sketchily, set up. You get oriented by visiting various rimpoches (teachers), each one a reincarnation of a spiritual figure, each one seated in his shrinelike cell, among tankas, flowers, bowls, rugs, lamps, and images.
>
> Each is seated at a particular plane, near or far. The Khempo of Namgyal high up on the mountain with his little community. Ratod Rimpoche just up the hill, near the official headquarters

of the Dalai Lama's administration. The little tulku higher up, just below the Khempo. And the Dalai Lama himself in a sort of center, where he is seated and guarded and fenced in.

Thus what was for me on Friday a rugged, non-descript mountain with a lot of miscellaneous dwellings, rocks, woods, farms, flocks, gulfs, falls and heights, is now spiritually ordered by permanent, seated presences, burning with a lamplike continuity and significance, centers of awareness and reminders of dharma (truth).

It is precisely this quality of seeing-through that participants in inter-faith exploration begin to develop, and it is learned more from immersion in prayer and contemplation than from theological debate. This is the value of the mystical traditions in each of the world's religions, much neglected in modern Western Christianity.

Merton was impressed with what he saw and experienced, but he was not trying to achieve a synthesis between Christianity and the Eastern traditions. He remained agnostic about whether mystics all experience the same Reality. Our very experience is itself conditioned by the possibilities extended to us in the spiritual traditions through which we grow. That is why in the end, he felt, we have to stay where we are. We have to penetrate through to the inner core of the faith we have already been given. When we do so, we may well find ourselves in the presence of unexpected and unfamiliar company. But we must begin from what we know.

Merton's example is merely one among many of Christians who have sought the "light of the East." Their witness has not been a defection to other religions, but a deepening of their own. Of perhaps even greater significance has been the witness of Asian Christians themselves. Those who have grown up within the culture of the East, as distinct from those who travel there from the West, bring a non-Western perspective to Christian theology and to inter-faith dialogue.

One of the most sublime and beautiful descriptions of the unity of religions comes from Christian Asia, from Indian-born Roman Catholic scholar Raimundo Panikkar. Using imagery drawn from nature, characteristic of Hindu writings, he describes a vision of the transcendent harmony of faiths.

The rivers of the earth do not actually meet each other, not even in the oceans, nor do they need to meet in order to be truly life-giving rivers.

But they do meet: they meet in the skies—that is, in heaven. The rivers do not meet, not even as water. They meet in the form of clouds, once they have suffered a transformation into vapour, which eventually will pour down again into the valleys of mortals to feed the rivers of the earth.

Religions do not coalesce, certainly not as organised religions. They meet once transformed into vapour, once metamorphosized into Spirit, which is then poured down in innumerable tongues.

The rivers are fed by descending clouds ... the true reservoir of religions lies not only in the doctrinal waters of theology; it lies also in the transcendental revelation of the divine clouds, and in the immanent inspiration from the glaciers and snow-laden mountains of the saints (*The Unknown Christ of Hinduism*, 1968).

Thus "sameness" among the world's religions is not the issue. Neither is uniqueness, for each tradition can claim that without contradiction. The real question raised by these explorers and bridge-builders is whether those of us who follow a particular spiritual path can discern the point within it at which its external forms become transparent to a deeper reality. Can we find that breakthrough point in our own faith journey beyond which there lies the possibility of an enormous spiritual freedom, deeper global understanding, and a more elevated communion with God?

Chapter 9

Grounded Openness

*A*nyone who advocates multi-religious dialogue and exploration within the church typically experiences two types of reaction. One is a welcoming interest. There is a recognition that people of other spiritual traditions are our neighbours, that there are potential benefits in better relationships for the whole religious community within society as well as for society itself. There may even be an admitted curiosity about other spiritual paths out of personal desire and interest, without any sense of betrayal or defection from Christian beliefs. The other is indifference or hostility. This may arise simply from lack of interest in the subject, or from a sense of threat posed by the proximity of racial and cultural aliens. But most often it comes from a deep conviction that one's commitment to Christian faith is weakened by openness to the beliefs of others, that "universalism" (the view that there are many paths to God) is un-Christian, that Jesus Christ is in fact the only way to salvation and that to believe otherwise is to deny the plain teaching of the Bible.

The first group would find the explorations of Thomas Merton and the visions of Raimundo Panikkar both enlightening and stimulating. The second would see them as a profound betrayal of truth, a fatal accommodation to liberalism and unbelief.

Why do we find such divergences within the church (or indeed within any religious tradition)? Why are there individuals willing to explore foreign countries and others insistent on staying at home? What differentiates those who feel it possible to remain a perfectly faithful Christian, while learning in depth from people of other religions, from those who do not?

Frithjof Schuon

These questions have been addressed in the writings of Frithjof Schuon, a Swiss philosopher who has been acclaimed as the greatest living authority on comparative religions. In 1993, in a book called *The Transcendent Unity of Religions,* Schuon proposed a theory both about religions and their followers that sheds some light on the kinds of responses we get from friends and fellow believers when this issue comes up.

First, he argues that there *is* a unity among the world's religions, but it is not a unity of common religious experience, or of dogma, or of either outward or inward nature. He acknowledges the differences among religions—having studied them intimately throughout his life—and says they are not only dissimilar in their external but also in their internal character. He argues, however, that the unity of religions consists in the point at which they all meet, the point beyond time and history and even beyond human knowledge at which the differences dissolve into a higher and ultimate Reality. He calls this the Transcendent. There is a transcendent unity among the world's religions.

His basis for this is the singular and unitary nature of the Transcendent itself. In Christian, Muslim, and Jewish language, God is one. In Hindu and even Buddhist language, the Pure Absolute is not differentiated, not plural in nature. All religions assert that at the heart of the universe there is one infinite and uncreated Reality, one Truth. Schuon's theory of religions is that they are the finite and relative vehicles by which this Truth is known by human beings—and also the means by which Truth knows itself.

> The whole debate regarding the capacity or the incapacity of the human mind to know God resolves itself thus: our intelligence can only know God "by God." Therefore it is God who knows Himself in us.

Why should God, who knows Himself in Himself, wish to know Himself also through man? Because, as a *hadith* (tradition) tells us, "I was a hidden treasure, and I wished to be known; hence I created the world" (*The Transcendent Unity of Religions*, 1993).

God is the hidden treasure at the heart of the universe who wishes to be known, and therefore creates the world and human beings with the capacity to comprehend our own eternal origin and end. The knowledge of God is not given through the intellect but through revelation, and revelation is specific to the culture and thought forms of the world's various peoples.

Each revelation is concrete, that is, mediated through certain familiar forms and outward appearances, and these differ from one form of the revelation to another. For this reason, religions coalesce and solidify around the concrete forms of their particular revelation. Hence, the knowledge of God can only come through commitment to particular forms and is not available universally or abstractly. There is properly, therefore, no such thing as "faith." There are only faiths.

Yet all knowledge is from the same source, claims Schuon. It all radiates from the same transcendent point. In his introduction to Schuon's book, Huston Smith draws a diagram to illustrate the idea.

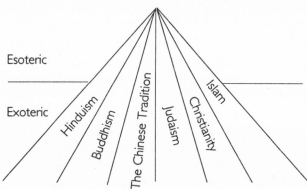

According to this theory, all religions meet in their origin and source. This transcendent Source is not available to our understanding directly, but only through mediating forms or appearances. Religion itself is one of those mediating forms, as well as the event or person that gives rise to it. While the forms of revelation are true representations of the divine, they are also intermediate. They are not the final Reality, which alone is God. This distinction is important, for it means that no particular form of divine revelation can be taken as ultimate or final, though they can be taken as true.

In Christianity, for example, God is made known to us through Jesus. And there is no dispute in Schuon's proposal that Jesus is the true revelation of God. He does not contest the description of Jesus in the New Testament that "He is the reflection of God's glory, the exact imprint of God's very being" (Heb. 1:3). Nor does he disagree with the same claim made by Hindus about the many incarnations of Vishnu, or with the Muslim belief that the divine will is fully revealed in the Koran. For he treats all of these forms as intermediate self-disclosures of the Absolute, which are necessarily final from the human standpoint but necessarily relative from God's.

The reason why revelation has to be mediated rather than direct, and multi-form rather than limited to one single demonstration, in Schuon's view, is that the human mind is incapable of receiving the Absolute in its pure essence. For our limited nature to be connected to the unmediated Absolute would be like connecting a light bulb directly to a nuclear power station. The result would be disastrous: "If Christ had been the only manifestation of the Word, supposing such a uniqueness of manifestation to be possible, the effect of His birth would have been the instantaneous reduction of the universe to ashes." Thus Schuon argues that a diversity of revelation from the divine to the human, the observed variety of the world's religions, is not only genuine but absolutely necessary. The world could not tolerate a single vehicle of access to the Absolute. It would destroy the fabric of creation.

Across the middle of the diagram illustrating the theory, Smith has drawn a line. This line points to a second and crucial aspect of Schuon's proposal. It has to do with two psychological states of religious awareness which, he believes, are commonly found in all spiritual seekers, and which he rather obscurely calls *exoteric* and *esoteric*. They have to do with seeing-as and seeing-through.

The exoteric believer is one for whom truth must be concrete and practical. This is a person who sees God in singular and unambiguous terms, and for whom the notion of a many-sided or multi-form revelation is meaningless and contradictory. This person's faith is grounded in specifics, in historical facts or in the distinct teachings of a particular faith community, and becomes insecure and tenuous if the anchors are pulled up and the vessel is set adrift. For the exoteric, abstractions and universalities have no grasp on the imagination or on the heart. The way in which God is known must therefore be the only way God can be known.

Esoterics, on the other hand, treat form as merely a vehicle for substance, albeit a necessary one. As in art or music, where a particular work may simply function as a window for the viewer through to a deeper and wider vista, the particular elements of religious faith are not of significance in themselves except as they reveal the hidden God within and behind them. The esoteric is drawn beyond the particular to the universal, the Absolute that transcends and relativizes the specific. This does not involve any denial of revelation. What the esoteric denies is the final character of any specific revelation, for in this state of awareness, historical and material distinctions are of little value. The ways in which God can be known are endless.

Huston Smith summarizes Schuon's two psychological types as follows:

> For the exoteric, God's personal mode is his only mode; for the esoteric this mode resides in one that is higher and ultimately modeless: the Absolute, the Godhead, Nirguna Brahman of the Vedantists, the Tao that cannot be spoken.
>
> For the exoteric the world is real in every sense; for the esoteric it has only qualified reality from the human standpoint and no separate reality whatsoever from the standpoint of the Godhead. The same holds for the human soul.
>
> For the exoteric, God is primarily loved; for the esoteric He is primarily known; though in the end the exoteric comes to know what he loves and the esoteric to love what he knows (*Transcendent Unity*, 1993).

To illustrate his point, Schuon discusses various passages from the Bible from both an exoteric and an esoteric point of view. The most difficult of these, as we have noted before, is Jesus' statement in John's gospel, "I am the Way, the Truth, and the Life. No one comes to the Father except by me" (14:6). To the exoteric, this is a clear indication that Jesus is the only and supreme manifestation of God. To the esoteric, it means that everyone who comes to God does so purely by God's own means. There is no genuine path to God that is not of God's creating.

> When we continue up the scale of extended meanings to "No man cometh to the Father except by me" men divide. For esoterics "me" will designate the Logos. For exoterics, less supple in their capacity for spiritual abstractions, in precise proportion as the word relaxes its hold on the concrete historical personage of Jesus of Nazareth, the assertion forfeits its saving power (*Transcendent Unity*, 1993).

Here we see the light that Schuon's interpretation sheds on inter-faith dialogue. The impasse we so often experience in debates within the church arises from our different psychological and spiritual awareness. Those for whom faith must be grounded in the concrete and specific will feel that all assertions of universalism must necessarily be untrue, or at best derivative. And those for whom the finite is simply a vehicle for the self-disclosure of the Infinite will resist all spiritual attachments and confinements that limit freedom of worship and contemplation. The difference between them has more to do with the subjective approach of the believer than the objective truth believed.

The same holds true for inter-faith discussions as well. People engaged in multi-faith encounter bring to it their own psychological and spiritual make-up. There is an exoteric-esoteric continuum in every gathering. Those who hold on securely to the explicit character of religion are often more interested in what makes one way of belief different from another. They are concerned with the distinctiveness of faith, its historical and concrete character. The mystically minded, on the other hand, are often more interested in the numinous aspects of religion, in learning what higher meanings are possible within each of the different traditions that binds them closer together. They seek the Truth that transcends the truth.

The point is, both exoterics and esoterics can be involved in inter-faith dialogue. Each brings what the other lacks. One group will ensure that the discussion remains grounded in tangible issues, in the actuality of life. The other will prevent the focus from being too narrow and material, and will take a longer view of the results. But both psychological types will have to start from a position of grounded openness.

Safe to Explore

Is it safe to wander far from home in spiritual matters? The question is legitimate, since there are demonic and destructive forms of religion waiting for the unwary traveller. There are new spiritual movements that have not yet demonstrated their authenticity, and revivals of older cultic ritualisms, such as Wicca, which are trying to emerge from under the weight of ancient denunciations to show that they were wrongly treated. There are also mind-possessing cults and evil satanic sects whose purpose is diabolical and whose methods are corrupt.

How safe is it to enter innocently into untested spiritual waters? A serious caution needs to be given here. Openness to a variety of religious practices is dangerous without the security of a grounded religious identity. You need to have a safe home in order to go travelling. You need to have deep spiritual roots before you can extend yourself into the unknown. Genuine inter-faith exploration is the work of deeply committed believers, not spiritual dilettantes. It is never about dabbling in the occult, or in the exotic, but rather about walking along other tried and proven paths with trusted and wise guides, all the time knowing how to get home.

Authentic exploration, therefore, is impossible without first belonging to a faith community. Or to put this another way, freedom arises from commitment. Those who are committed to religious faith make the best partners in dialogue. Those who are uncommitted may well have the quality of openness that dialogue requires, but they lack the rootedness without which dialogue dissipates into meaninglessness.

Grounded openness is the quality we see in all the great pioneers of inter-religious understanding. It is an evident characteristic of Jesus, for example. His contacts with men and women of other religious traditions in the gospels illustrate both his own deep self-knowledge and his radical commitment to love and justice beyond the boundaries of religious or tribal identification. In his relationships with the Gentiles, the Samaritans, and with the Syro-Phoenician woman (Matt. 15:22–28), Jesus maintained the position of a faithful Jew, never surrendering his position for the sake of compromise, but always extending the divine love to everyone who demonstrated genuine hope in God.

In fact, Jesus reserved his greatest criticism for the "orthodox" believers of his day, whose narrow rigidities blinded them to the fullness of God's grace in the world. He called them snakes, hypocrites, painted tombs! There is no gentleness at all in Jesus' language about those who use religion to place burdens on others and to erect barriers against the freedom of God's Spirit. Those who assume the mantle of orthodoxy today in order to attack the faith of others need to beware. Jesus was much more patient with those who were open but not grounded (like the rich young ruler in Luke 18) than with the religious bigots who were grounded but not open to the grace of God.

Grounded openness is a posture of discernment, of critical and discriminating participation in the possibility of grace within the unfamiliar. It is an attitude of bringing what we know of God into relationship with what others have fruitfully experienced. This is not the same thing as romantic idealism or spiritual naïveté. It means, in the words of the New Testament, "testing the spirits to see whether they are of God" (1 John 4:1). If the same divine source is the origin of genuine spiritual knowledge, then we may expect to find a ring of truth in authentic piety, however foreign. We shall be able to find connections with truth under the guidance of the Spirit. And we shall discard whatever violates our forbearance or denies what we know in Christ.

This same posture towards others has to be taken towards ourselves. Grounded openness is equally self-critical. There are always elements in our own understanding that limit our faithfulness to God, and sometimes these only become apparent when we look in upon ourselves through a new window. There may be things within Christianity we might come to deny, confessional statements we feel must be jettisoned under the impact of new insights and learning.

Inter-faith dialogue often produces a new self-awareness that is both affirming and denying of formerly accepted beliefs. It may challenge us to move into politically unsafe areas of theological creativity or new doctrinal formulation out of the desire to pursue God's unfolding revelation. And yet the potential rewards of these risks are worthy of noble spirits. New Zealand scholar Peter Donovan writes,

> One feature especially characterizes inter-religious encounters, whether they are formally organised between official representatives, or impromptu meetings between lay people. It is a shared sense of standing together on "holy ground," a recognition that awesome issues are at stake, awesome risks being taken.
>
> For almost without exception each participant can be found representing one or more of the great divisive forces of our world—race, culture, power, territory, ideology. All can find, in their national and often in their own personal histories, memories of involvement in oppression, persecution, genocide, slavery, terrorism, hatred and enmity—whether as guilty parties or as sufferers at the hands of others.
>
> What their experience bears witness to, above all, is a tremendous capacity for forgiveness and generosity of spirit— often emanating from those who have suffered the most wrong at the hands of others. This capacity, this power for peace-making and acceptance, is perceived to be more than of human origin. It is recognised as a blessing, a gift from God (*Experience in Inter-Religious Dialogue*, 1991).

While consternation about inter-faith exploration is understandable, and is clarified by Schuon's distinction between spiritual and psychological types, it is nevertheless not really faithful. No genuinely faithful person can limit the grace and blessing of God or deny its presence to others. Faith itself requires a charitableness of both the heart and the mind. Authentic belief does not require us to resist the promptings of charity.

Chapter 10

Drawing the Circle Wider

Viewed historically, Christianity has evolved and developed dramatically since its beginnings as a Jewish sect. It is impossible to claim that the faith of the apostles has been handed down unchanged across twenty centuries of human civilization. We do not believe today in the same way as people did in the first century of the Christian era, whatever our assumed orthodoxy might be. Neither did the Jews of Jesus' time believe in the same way as their ancestors who founded the nation of Israel after wandering forty years in the wilderness.

There is a natural and necessary evolution in human thought and believing, though this is not to claim any superficial theory of human progress. What is remarkable about this development in the Christian tradition is how each stage of it has enlarged the religious imagination of the faithful. At each of the seminal moments of our evolving, there has been a discernible expansion of spiritual understanding, as if God is drawing us into larger and larger circles of seeing. We can trace this process right through the Bible itself.

From Polytheism to Monotheism

It is important to remember that the Bible is not a book but a collection of writings covering almost a thousand years of religious history in one small part of the world. It reveals, above all, an evolving understanding of God by the people of one nation through dramatically changing circumstances over many centuries. This evolution of religious understanding is evident to any student of the Bible. There is no single and uniform concept of God throughout Scripture. What we find there is an evolution of theological understanding that moves from pluralistic polytheism to universal monotheism—that is, from belief in many local gods, of whom Jahweh was but one, to a sense of one universal Sovereign, the Creator of all, the judge and ruler of every nation on the face of the earth.

We may call this process an *emerging God-consciousness,* a gradual drawing of the circle of divine knowledge wider and wider through encounter with the sheer vastness of the mystery of God. It was not that the nature of God changed in this period. Rather, people came to ever new understandings of the divine as they encountered God's redemptive presence in their life and sufferings over a long and often bitter history.

An important early stage in this process was the covenant with Moses. After their deliverance from slavery in Egypt, the newly freed Hebrew tribes were bound to a special relationship with God through the covenant. They were to be a "chosen" people, a people set apart by God's decree as "a light to the nations." Jahweh would be their God, and they would be Jahweh's people. The law of Moses and the land of Israel were signs of this covenant bond, and they endure to this day.

Out of this covenant relationship, there arose from time to time a sense of uniqueness, a self-understanding based on a divinely appointed status. In early biblical history, it was believed that Israel was a protected land, that no harm would come to its occupants, that God was on the side of the nation. Trouble, whenever it disturbed the kingdom, was blamed on the waywardness of rulers, or on the people themselves, and religious reforms would reinstate the traditional cultic and ritual practices of former times. But it was never considered—with the exception of solitary prophetic voices—that the nation could be destroyed.

Then in the sixth century B.C.E. came the shattering experience of the Exile. The Temple in Jerusalem was destroyed, the land was razed, and the people were carried off into slavery again. It is hard to overstate the spiritual impact of the Exile on the religious self-understanding of the Jews. It was as if everything they had believed about God and their special status had been negated. How could God uphold the cause of another nation against their own? What did God mean by saying, "I will be your God and you will be my people"? Not only the nation was destroyed, but along with it the entire self-understanding of the faithful. By the waters of Babylon they sat down and wept. They were in profound turmoil for years and years.

It was the prophets of the Exile—Second Isaiah, Jeremiah, and Ezekiel—who helped them survive the spiritual and theological crisis. These prophets taught the people that God had not abandoned them. Rather, God had judged them. Babylon was merely the tool that had been used to purify them and to break their hearts of stone. With the teaching of the prophets came a new realization about God and the meaning of the covenant. God, they now saw, is no tribal deity, no private national sponsor, but the lord of all the nations. And this God is a just God, whose judgement is to be feared and whose ways are to be followed. The covenant with Israel was no longer seen as a special privilege, but as a special responsibility—to proclaim this God of justice to all people, and to demonstrate the path of righteousness so that all might live in peace and truth.

There is no doubt that this major development in religious understanding, created by the political crisis of conquest, helped biblical religion to evolve from polytheism to monotheism. It brought about a radically new and self-critical awareness that spiritual faithfulness cannot be reduced to the mere performance of religious rituals, as if God's majesty requires no more than merely outward and symbolic recognition. The great prophets of this period shifted the ground of religious understanding from ritualism to ethics—from the belief that God desires correct worship to the realization that God demands global justice and righteousness.

Both Amos and Isaiah thundered against tribal and elitist doctrines of God and proposed instead a vision of a cosmic Sovereign whose favour is upon those who do good in every nation. "Let justice roll down like a mighty river," urged Amos—a cry that has been repeated throughout the world whenever cruelty and suffering has been ignored by religious people. "I hate, I despise your fasts," warned Isaiah. "Is not this the fast that I choose: to loose the bonds of injustice, to undo the thongs of the yoke, to let the oppressed go free, and to break every yoke? Is it not to share your bread with the hungry, and bring the homeless poor into your house?" (58:6-7) Thus, biblical religion lays the groundwork for the reform and correction of any tradition claiming its authority that neglects or encourages injustice, pride, and intolerance.

A further important development took place in the post-exilic period. As religious understanding moved beyond tribalism and nationalism to a sense of God's universal sovereignty, and from ritualism in narrow terms to the global imperatives of justice and love, there arose the profound and disturbing question of human suffering. This is a question that arises perpetually in all religious traditions, and that constitutes for many the greatest single difficulty with religious belief. It is a profoundly human question, and in the Bible it is examined with searing honesty in the book of Job.

Job is a deep and breathtaking exploration of the problem of innocent suffering. The story and its aftermath challenge all simplistic notions of evil and injustice, especially those that offer ingenuous cause-and-effect explanations for human misery. Why do the innocent suffer? Why does tragedy strike the righteous, the weak, the young, the most defenceless? The question is raised with particular sharpness precisely because of the biblical insistence on God's righteousness and its claim that God shows favour to all who act justly in every nation. Job presents the case of a man who did act justly, who did live an ethical life, and who honoured God not only with his lips but in his deeds. His undeserved misery and abject suffering constitute a fundamental case against the ethics of God, and for this reason Job is of immense significance in the biblical tradition.

The book examines and systematically discards the usual explanations for suffering—the theory of Just Deserts, for example, which suggests people deserve their lot in life, or the notion that God is good only to those whose theology and worship is doctrinally and ritually correct. The case for these theories is made by Job's comforters, his friends who turn up to help him understand what he must have done wrong. The narrative devastates these arguments, and leaves us in the end with no explanation at all for the problem of evil, the seeming randomness of human misfortune that strikes the deserving and the undeserving alike with frightening irrationality. Job culminates with a climactic, almost terrifying, description of God's power and sovereignty over the whole cosmos, which relativizes and minimizes the centrality of human experience.

It is a matter even today of intense debate whether Job ever received an answer to his question, and if so what sort of answer it was. But the enduring witness of the book is to the essentially mysterious nature of God, to the utter impenetrability of the divine in human terms, and away from confining theories that limit God's nature to any finite system of belief or any criterion of human experience. If the prophets shifted the religious axis from ritual to ethics, Job shifts it again to mystery, awe, and sheer belief, despite all the odds.

Thus we find in Hebrew religion, over five hundred years before the emergence of Christianity, a tradition that challenges notions of spiritual elitism and extends the notion of God's favour to include everyone who practises justice and seeks to do what is right, a tradition that warns the spiritually unwary against any attempt to claim final or ultimate understanding of the nature of God.

This is the tradition that gave birth to the New Testament. The early Christian church, as well as the historical Jesus of Nazareth, were born into this Jewish theological perspective. Jesus stood unambiguously within the prophetic tradition of Amos, Isaiah, and Job. He challenged the adequacy of legalistic notions of righteousness. He countered—along with other Jewish teachers—strict views of the Sabbath that condemned any act of compassion or justice even when the situation clearly required it (Mark 2:27), and he refused to support the idea that people were afflicted with suffering because of sin (John 9:1–9). Jesus summoned people constantly beyond the temptation to domesticate and reduce God into something manageable, predictable, and tribal, and he had little patience with those who insisted upon the letter of Scripture in violation of God's indiscriminate love. He invited people to give up everything, not simply their material possessions but their spiritual limitations as well, and to follow him.

With Jesus, the biblical doctrine of God unfolds again. Not only did he demonstrate great respect for people of other religions like Samaritans and Gentiles, he also savagely attacked retrenched religious leadership and the teachings of blind guides. Though he was a faithful Jew, he appears not to have been concerned with propositional faith and its doctrinal implications so much as with making possible a new way of life for those who followed him. In their later reflection on his life, death and resurrection, early Christians came to the view that in Christ God had made a new covenant—a covenant not simply with the people of Israel but with all humanity. It was further suggested that there had been a cosmic dimension to his reconciling work, that God was making a new creation and that the old order of reality itself had passed away.

The implications of this new covenant in Jesus Christ take our God-consciousness even further. In Christ, God has taken a decisive new initiative and enlarged the promise of salvation to include not simply chosen people but all people. The good news of the new covenant is that *all people are now chosen people.* "There is no longer Jew nor Greek, male nor female, slave nor free, but all are one in Christ Jesus" (Gal. 3:28). Thus, early Christians believed that God had established a new Israel, a new global community through faith in Jesus Christ. We are now very far indeed from the limited and strictly local deity of the early biblical tradition—the Jahweh of the Ark of the Covenant, for instance, whom the faithful carried into battle in a box.

Thus we may say that, within the pages of the Bible itself, we see a gradual development in the doctrine of God, an evolution from tribalism to universality, from pluralistic polytheism to inclusive monotheism. The circle keeps getting wider. Its orbit sweeps more and more people into its vision. It is a gradually but inexorably enlarging idea whose dimensions keep resisting cultural and doctrinal confinement. It is not that God gets larger as we move from Genesis to Revelation, but that the religious imagination is impelled further and further outwards under the very dynamism of God's self-disclosure.

Jewish and Christian traditions diverge at this point. Though springing from common origins in their early Hebrew roots, Judaism and Christianity have followed different historical paths. Each has continued to evolve in its separate theological and spiritual character. Never confined to a written scriptural tradition, Judaism has been enriched by an oral tradition and by the development of authorities like Talmud, Midrash, and Halakhah. Yet for Christianity, this is where the Bible stops. Unlike the Hebrew writings, the New Testament spans a mere sixty years. There is no scriptural development past this point, nor could there have been. The church itself limited the canon of Scripture to those apostolic writings belonging to the first century in the Christian era.

This raises the question of whether biblical Christianity is incapable of further development with respect to other religious traditions. Do the limitations of Scripture create an impassable boundary for adherents of biblical religion?

Beyond Scripture

We must remember that in the apostolic period, many in the Jewish community regarded the Christian sect as heretics, as misguided and deluded nonconformists. In the early years there were attempts to repress the new Christian teaching as blasphemy and error, although these efforts were condemned by senior Jewish leaders like Gamaliel (Acts 5:34–39). Later, hostility and persecutions arose from the Gentile world as well, and there were serious internal disputes that threatened the unity and cohesion of the fledgling movement. The church was small and threatened on many fronts. It is therefore all the more remarkable that the Christian vision of global/cosmic redemption won by Jesus Christ survived and prospered against all opportunities for its demise.

But it survived by crystallizing itself into an absolutist theology, a gospel so firmly Christocentric that it could not yet contemplate the possibility of other ways of redemption. As David Lochhead observes, absolutist positions are generally the product of a climate of hostility and danger, when the power of one community threatens the beliefs of another. Christian exclusivism in the New Testament clearly has its origins here, in the efforts of the apostolic community to differentiate itself from other dominant forces that rejected its claims about Jesus Christ.

Today, if we take the view that all human understanding of God stops with the New Testament, that nothing new has been revealed since the writer of Revelation laid down his pen, that all knowledge of God ceases with Jesus Christ, then we must remain with either an exclusivist or an inclusivist attitude to the other great religions of the world. This is the position of perhaps the majority of Christians today.

If, however, we take the view that the growth of God-consciousness need not end with Jewish-Christians of the first century, that new understanding is possible and indeed necessary for world peace and survival, then we may feel ourselves impelled towards a yet wider view of God's self-disclosure. This would, in my view, be entirely consistent with Scriptural tradition taken as a whole and with the God of love made manifest in Jesus Christ. It would be faithful to the pattern, already evident in the Bible, of historical evolution in human understanding of God, an ever-widening circle of knowledge based on the core foundation of the old and new covenants between God and Israel. It would not deny the central witness of Scripture to a universally sovereign Lord whose will it is that all people should be saved, but rather take that witness to its next logical step.

Just as the new covenant in Christ was not a betrayal by God of the earlier covenant with Israel—not a betrayal but a fulfilment of it in Christian understanding—so it may also be a fulfilment of that same Gospel to proclaim God's presence in other historic religions of the world: to suggest boldly that divine grace may be experienced through other religious paths without any contradiction of the way of salvation offered in Jesus Christ.

Perhaps it is time for us to see that the same God who kept challenging and judging the limited understanding of earlier generations of believers, and brought about an ever new and ever larger knowledge of the grace and power of salvation in human history, is now challenging and judging our own limited historic exclusivism as Christians, and is calling us to broaden further our belief in the possibilities for human redemption.

What the Bible proclaims with consistent clarity is a God who creates all humanity in the divine image and seeks our restoration to wholeness and fullness of life through revelation and grace. This is a universal proclamation, even though it is mediated and revealed within particulars.

In fact, the very dynamic of Scripture itself compels us to move beyond it in order to be faithful to the God it reveals. The church has always claimed the freedom to do this when the Holy Spirit has led

Christians to revise their earlier beliefs and practices. Thus we have dramatically altered our views on such things as the divine right of kings, slavery, animal sacrifices, the lending of money for profit, the beating of children, the role of women, divorce, and pacifism—all of which are enjoined by Scripture in a way Christians no longer regard as normative today. Christian attitudes to these things have changed not in violation of God's Word but in response to it. The same Spirit that inspired the writers of Scripture also inspires the church in the act of interpretation and in discernment of God's continuing revelation.

It is therefore important to see that the new global context of religious and cultural pluralism requires new acts of biblical interpretation. The ancient world that produced the epistles and gospels was not facing the situation we face today. Its answers to those questions are not necessarily answers to our questions.

Bishop Kenneth Cragg writes,

> The land of Sinim—China—finds a mention in Isaiah (49:12), but there is no encounter with Confucius. From Midian and Sheba to Tarshish and the isles is the range of the Old Testament. The New Testament is all around the Mediterranean, but no further.
>
> There are no letters of Paul to the Meccans.
>
> This limitation of our canonical frame of reference has to be taken seriously and is not made good by isolated quotation, whether "exclusivist" or "inclusivist." It may be that the meaning of the Holy Spirit is that we have to take extra-canonical liberties (*To Meet and To Greet*, 1994).

This taking of liberties beyond the Bible is not an act of irresponsibility, but rather a responsiveness to the God who is revealed among the religions of the world. It is to respect the universal sovereignty of One who is always greater than our limited perceptions and cultural particularities.

Whose Salvation Is It?

Moving beyond the Bible will require of us, paradoxically, a new agnosticism. I mean by this a suspension of judgement on the whole question of who is, and who is not, to be saved in the final judgement of God. Bishop Lesslie Newbigin has put this very well:

How are we to regard the other commitments, faiths, worldviews to which people around us and with whom we live and move adhere?

I believe the debate about this question has been fatally flawed by the fact that it has been conducted around the question, "Who can be saved?" It has been taken for granted that the only question was "Can the good non-Christian be saved?..."Where will she go when she dies?"...There has been an almost unquestioned assumption that the only question is "What happens to the non-Christian after death?"

I want to affirm that this is the wrong question and that as long as it remains the central question we shall never come to the truth. And this for three reasons:

a) First and simply, it is the wrong question because it is a question to which God alone has the right to give an answer. I confess that I am astounded at the arrogance of theologians who seem to think that we are authorized, in our capacity as Christians, to inform the rest of the world about who is to be vindicated and who is to be condemned at the last judgement.

b) Second, because it is based on an abstraction. By concentrating on the fate of the individual soul after death, it abstracts the soul from the full reality of the human person as an actor and sufferer in the ongoing history of the world... Our dialogue with people of other faiths must be about what is happening in the world now and about how we understand it and take part in it. It cannot be only, or even mainly, about our destiny as individual souls after death.

c) Third, because this way of putting the question starts with the individual and his or her need to be assured of ultimate happiness, and not with God and his glory.. This is a perversion of the gospel. For anyone who has understood what God has done for us all in Jesus Christ, the one question is "How shall God be glorified? How shall his amazing grace be known and celebrated and adored?"

Christian faith is skewed if it begins with the question "Who is going to be saved at the end?" That is a question which God alone will answer, and it is an arrogant presumption on the part of theologians to suppose it is their business to answer it. We have to begin with the mighty work of God in Jesus Christ and ask, "How is he to be honoured and glorified?" (*The Gospel in a Pluralist Society*, 1989).

This agnosticism about the recipients of salvation is essentially biblical. Jesus consistently refused to be drawn into discussion about who would or would not be saved in the afterlife. When some Sadducees (who did not believe in an afterlife) attempted to engage Jesus in an argument about it (Matt: 22:23–33), our Lord responded by dismissing their efforts and scoffing at their projections of the present order of reality into the great beyond. Similarly, when an anxious mother wanted to ensure the future for her sons well beyond not only their infancy and adulthood, but their earthly life itself (Matt: 20:20-23), Jesus replied that such disposition was not his to give but belonged solely to the Father in heaven. Over and over again, we find Jesus turning back the natural but errant questioning of his followers about the recipients of salvation. This is for God alone to decide.

What about Evangelism?

A Christian is, by definition, one who knows—or at least is travelling along—the path of salvation through Jesus Christ. Nothing of what has been written here should be taken as a denial or relativizing of the truth of Christ. "We speak of what we have heard and seen" says the first letter of John (1:1), and that must always remain the position of the Christian in inter-faith dialogue. All genuine dialogue involves testimony to what we know and believe. There can be no dialogue without an authentic sharing and proclamation of the truth that has brought us into God's kingdom.

This means that evangelism, in the true sense of the word, must unavoidably be a part of inter-faith dialogue. Evangelism is sharing the gospel of Jesus Christ with all who have ears to hear and eyes to see. Evangelism is not the same as proselytism, which has no place in dialogue. Dialogue for the Christian necessarily involves a deep personal commitment to the gospel and to the person and work of Jesus. There is no point in dialogue with someone who is not committed to his or her religion. No self-respecting Jew, Muslim, or Hindu wants to be engaged in discussion with a soft-minded Christianity unable to take its own side in debate. But neither is dialogue possible among fundamentalists or those whose vision of truth excludes everyone but themselves. What I am arguing for is a commitment among Christians to a gospel that compels us beyond fundamentalism to see in other religions the God we know in Jesus Christ, and a willingness to encounter God in other traditions in ways that may transform the understanding of our own tradition.

A Christian is one who believes Jesus Christ to be the way, the truth, and the life. This is not to say there are no others. It is to say simply that it is the one we know. And for this reason it is the path we must follow and invite others along. Christian commitment to truth requires us to avoid the falsification of others' beliefs. It is not necessary to bear false witness against our neighbour in order to bear true witness to Christ. Therefore we must avoid the constant temptation to point to the negative and destructive aspects of others' belief systems and ignore the same elements in our own. It is wrong to compare the best of Christianity with the worst of Judaism, Islam, etc. Such approaches are self-serving and rightly deserve condemnation.

By the same token, we are bound to oppose in all religions—our own included—all that diminishes and negates the majesty of God and the well-being of God's people. We can say without reservation that we must be against whatever denies the gospel, whether in Christianity as it has been taught or in some other tradition. Poverty, violence, slavery, all forms of human degradation, the destruction of our carefully balanced ecosystems, personal and systemic sinfulness, corporate and individual evil, and every kind of religious bigotry and prejudice. An openness to the world's great spiritual pathways does not allow us to sanctify iniquity and wickedness in our own or in anyone else's religion. Tolerance must of necessity exclude intolerance. For Christians, Jesus Christ is and must remain the non-negotiable criterion of truth.

And yet we must take great care not to limit our faith in Jesus to any narrow dogmatism or blind uncritical creed. Too many of us have made Jesus into an idol, a false god who is created in our own image. Bishop Frank Griswold of Chicago has used the term "Jesusolatry" to describe the limiting of Christ to an exclusivist icon. This distorts the gospel and turns Jesus into an end rather than a means of God's grace and love. It is important to remember that Christ is "other" than us, transcendent, glorified, not to be confused with any human project or construct or, perhaps in the end, with any religion. Christ stands over against all our human systems of thought and belief and can never be captured by them.

"Enter by the narrow gate," Jesus once said (Matt: 7:13). But this narrow gate leads to a wide and expansive region of the soul, a vast encompassing vision of the love of God poured out upon the whole creation. It is surely not a narrow gate leading to an even narrower territory beyond, though it may yet be true, as Jesus said, that there are few who find it. Religious believers can be so dangerously and rigidly committed to defiant absolutisms. The idea that others may share in the inheritance given to them alone appears to many as manifestly unfair. Yet this is clearly what Jesus had in mind in the parable about vineyard workers receiving the same pay for different work (Matt: 20:1–16). The wisdom of God is such folly to those who resent magnanimity.

What does this mean for the evangelism of non-believers? I suggest it means we should lose no opportunity to witness to our faith in Christ among those who have no faith at all. As a religious pluralist, I am still obliged to witness to my faith in Jesus Christ. I cannot be on all paths at once. I must proclaim boldly the one I am on. But there are millions of people in our society who are on no path at all, or on a destructive, perhaps even demonic, path and have lost their way altogether. There are millions in our own society, in our own neighbourhoods and workplaces, who have no knowledge of God, no assurance of love, no spiritual path—whether Christian or other—to give them hope in the midst of life's suffering. These are more worthy subjects of our evangelistic concern. Evangelism should be directed towards those who have no living faith, not those who do.

There will always be movement of individuals from one religion to another, of course. For this we should be neither triumphant nor bitter. God calls each of us in God's own way. It is not for us to determine in which mansion of God's kingdom each individual will reside. The mission of the church is to build God's kingdom of peace and justice. It is not to destroy other cultures and peoples.

Why then be a Christian at all? Why bother with Jesus if there is more than one pathway to God? The answer can only be that Christianity is a true and authentic faith, and Jesus Christ a sure and certain Saviour. Any who seek the fullness of life, any who desire to be rescued from broken lives of sin and self-concern, all who long for pardon, forgiveness, hope and joy, need only turn to him and God will do the rest. "All who look to me will be saved," promises the Christ of John's gospel. There is no need to doubt his word, nor to deny it to those who profess faith in other ways.

I believe this is what Jesus requires of us today. Not imperialism in his name, but love and justice. Not conquest of other religions but mutual respect and tolerance. Not superiority but humility. There is real urgency in this task. But it is not an urgency to make the whole world Christian. Rather, it is to address the suffering of humanity, the tragedy and chaos, the destitution and hopelessness with which God's people struggle daily. To do this, we must respect religious differences and recognize that the true work of Christ is not in correcting other people's theology but in healing their wounds and raising them up in hope of new life. It requires of us a new spirit of tolerance and generosity. We have much to repent of, and we have much to be proud of. We have as our head the Prince of Peace. Let us be peaceable builders of his kingdom.

Appendix A

Statements of the Lambeth Conference on Other Religions

1897 (Resolution 15)

That the tendency of many English-speaking Christians to entertain an exaggerated opinion of the excellences of Hinduism and Buddhism, and to ignore the fact that Jesus Christ alone has been constituted Saviour and King of mankind, should be vigorously corrected.

1920 (Resolution 41)

In dealing with the large number of persons in their colonies and dependencies who profess different faiths, the policy of the British and American governments has always been that of strict religious neutrality. We heartily endorse this policy, having no desire to see any political influence brought to bear upon people to induce them to change their religion.

[However] ... we feel it is necessary to urge that the religious sentiments of Christians are entitled to be treated with the same consideration that is so markedly, and rightly, shown to those men professing other faiths.

1920 (Resolution 55)

We reaffirm our conviction that the revelation of God in Christ Jesus is the supreme and sufficient message given to all mankind, whereby we may attain to eternal life. We recognize that modern movements of thought connected with spiritualism, Christian Science, and theosophy join with the Christian Church in protesting against a materialistic view of the universe and at some points emphasize partially neglected aspects of truth.

At the same time, we feel bound to call attention to the fact that both in the underlying philosophy and in cults and practices which have arisen out of these movements, the teaching given or implied either ignores or explains away or contradicts the unique and central fact of human history, namely, the incarnation of our Lord and Saviour Jesus Christ.

1968 (Resolution 11)

It is the conviction of the Conference that, in obedience to Christ's mission and command and in their obligation towards the contemporary world, the Christian Churches must endeavour such positive relationship to the different religions of men, and to the doubt and denial of faith, as will:

a) set forward the common unity of mankind and a common participation in its present history;

b) encourage Christians to increasing cooperation with men of other faiths in the fields of economic, social, and moral action;

c) call Christians not only to study other faiths in their own seriousness, but also to study unbelief in its real quality.

1968 (Resolution 12)

The Conference recommends a renewed and vigorous implementation of the task of inter-religious dialogue already set in hand in the study centres organized by the World Council of Churches and other bodies, and urges increased Anglican support both in the seconding of personnel and in the provision of money. It also commends similar assistance for dialogue with Marxists and those who profess no religious faith.

1978 (Resolution 37)

1. Within the Church's trust of the Gospel, we recognize and welcome the obligation to open exchange of thought and experience with people of other faiths. Sensitivity to the work of the Holy Spirit among them means a positive response to their meaning as inwardly lived and understood. It means also a quality of life on our part which expresses the truth and love of God as we have known them in Christ, Lord and Saviour.

2. We realize the lively vocation to theological interpretation, community involvement, social responsibility, and evangelization which is carried by the Churches in areas where Hinduism, Buddhism, Taoism, Confucianism, and Islam are dominant, and ask that the whole Anglican Communion support them by understanding, by prayer, and where appropriate, by partnership with them.

3. We continue to seek opportunities for dialogue with Judaism.

1988 (Resolution 20)

This Conference commends dialogue with people of other faiths as part of Christian discipleship and mission, with the understanding that:

1) dialogue begins when people meet each other;
2) dialogue depends upon mutual understanding, mutual respect, and mutual trust;
3) dialogue makes it possible to share in service to the community;
4) dialogue becomes a medium of authentic witness.

Acknowledging that such dialogue, which is not a substitute for evangelism, may be a contribution in helping people of different faiths to make common cause in resolving issues of peacemaking, social justice and religious liberty, we further commend each province to initiate such dialogue in partnership with other Christian Churches where appropriate.

Appendix B

Towards a Global Ethic

Parliament of the World's Religions
Chicago, Illinois, 1993

The world is in agony. The agony is so pervasive and urgent that we are compelled to name its manifestations so that the depth of this pain may be made clear.

Peace eludes us ... the planet is being destroyed ... neighbours live in fear ... women and men are estranged from each other ... children die!

This is abhorrent!

We condemn the abuses of Earth's ecosystems.

We condemn the poverty that stifles life's potential; the hunger that weakens the human body; the economic disparities that threaten so many families with ruin. We condemn the social disarray of the nations; the disregard for justice which pushes citizens to the margin; the anarchy overtaking our communities; and the insane death of children from violence. In particular we condemn aggression in the name of religion.

But this agony need not be.

It need not be because the basis for an ethic already exists. This ethic offers the possibility of a better individual and global order, and leads individuals away from despair and societies away from chaos.

We are women and men who have embraced the precepts and practices of the world's religions:

We affirm that a common set of core values is found in the teachings of the religions, and that these form the basis of a global ethic.

We affirm that this truth is already known, but yet to be lived in heart and action.

We affirm that there is an irrevocable, unconditional norm for all areas of life, for families and communities, for races, nations, and religions. There already exist ancient guidelines for human behaviour which are found in the teachings of the religions of the world and which are the condition for a sustainable world order.

We Declare:

We are interdependent. Each of us depends on the well-being of the whole, and so we have respect for the community of living beings, for people, animals, and plants, and for the preservation of Earth, the air, water and soil.

We take individual responsibility for all we do. All our decisions, actions, and failures to act have consequences.

We must treat others as we wish others to treat us. We make a commitment to respect life and dignity, individuality and diversity, so that every person is treated humanely, without exception. We must have patience and acceptance. We must be able to forgive, learning from the past but never allowing ourselves to be enslaved by memories of hate. Opening our hearts to one another, we must sink our narrow differences for the cause of the world community, practising a culture of solidarity and relatedness.

We consider humankind our family. We must strive to be kind and generous. We must not live for ourselves alone, but should also serve others, never forgetting the children, the aged, the poor, the suffering, the disabled, the refugees, and the lonely. No person should ever be considered or treated as a second-class citizen, or be exploited in any way whatsoever. There should be equal partnership between men and women. We must not commit any kind of sexual immorality. We must put behind us all forms of domination or abuse.

We commit ourselves to a culture of non-violence, respect, justice, and peace. We shall not oppress, injure, torture, or kill other human beings, forsaking violence as a means of settling differences.

We must strive for a just social and economic order, in which everyone has an equal chance to reach full potential as a human being. We must speak and act truthfully and with compassion, dealing fairly with all, and avoiding prejudice and hatred. We must not steal. We must move beyond the dominance of greed for power, prestige, money, and consumption to make a just and peaceful world.

Earth cannot be changed for the better unless the consciousness of individuals is changed first. We pledge to increase our awareness by disciplining our minds, by meditation, by prayer, or by positive thinking. Without risk and a readiness to sacrifice there can be no fundamental change in our situation. Therefore we commit ourselves to this global ethic, to understanding one another, and to socially-beneficial, peace-fostering, and nature-friendly ways of life.

We invite all people, whether religious or not, to do the same.

The Principles of a Global Ethic

Our world is experiencing a fundamental crisis: A crisis in global economy, global ecology, and global politics. The lack of a grand vision, the tangle of unresolved problems, political paralysis, mediocre political leadership with little insight or foresight, and in general too little sense for the commonweal are seen everywhere: Too many old answers to new challenges.

Hundreds of millions of human beings on our planet increasingly suffer from unemployment, poverty, hunger, and the destruction of their families. Hope for a lasting peace among nations slips away from us. There are tensions between the sexes and generations. Children die, kill, and are killed. More and more countries are shaken by corruption in politics and business. It is increasingly difficult to live together peacefully in our cities because of social, racial, and ethnic conflicts, the abuse of drugs, organized crime, and even anarchy.

Even neighbours often live in fear of one another. Our planet continues to be ruthlessly plundered. A collapse of the ecosystem threatens us.

Time and again we see leaders and members of religions incite aggression, fanaticism, hate, and xenophobia—even inspire and legitimate violent and bloody conflicts. Religion often is misused for purely power-political goals, including war. We are filled with disgust.

We condemn these blights and declare that they need not be. An ethic already exists within the religious teachings of the world which can counter the global distress. Of course this ethic provides no direct solution for all the immense problems of the world, but it does supply the moral foundation for a better individual and global order: A vision which can lead women and men away from despair, and society away from chaos.

We are persons who have committed ourselves to the precepts and practices of the world religions. We confirm that there is already a consensus among the religions which can be the basis for a global ethic—a minimal *fundamental consensus concerning binding values, irrevocable standards,* and *fundamental moral attitudes.*

I. No new global order without a new global ethic!

We women and men of various religions and regions of Earth therefore address all people, religious and non-religious. We wish to express the following convictions which we hold in common:

We all have a responsibility for a better global order.

Our involvement for the sake of human rights, freedom, justice, peace, and the preservation of Earth is absolutely necessary.

Our different religious and cultural traditions must not prevent our common involvement in opposing all forms of inhumanity and working for greater humaneness.

The principles expressed in this Global Ethic can be affirmed by all persons with ethical convictions, whether religiously grounded or not.

As religious and spiritual persons we base our lives on an Ultimate Reality, and draw spiritual power and hope therefrom, in trust, in prayer or meditation, in word or silence. We have a special responsibility for the welfare of all humanity and care for the planet Earth. We do not consider ourselves better than other women and men, but we trust that the ancient wisdom of our religions can point the way for the future.

After two world wars and the end of the cold war, the collapse of fascism and nazism, the shaking to the foundations of communism and colonialism, humanity has entered a new phase of its history. Today we possess sufficient economic, cultural, and spiritual resources to introduce a better global order. But old and new ethnic, national, social, economic, and religious tensions threaten the peaceful building of a better world. We have experienced greater technological progress than ever before, yet we see that worldwide poverty, hunger, death of children, unemployment, misery, and the destruction of nature have not diminished but rather have increased. Many peoples are threatened with economic ruin, social disarray, political marginalization, ecological catastrophe, and national collapse.

In such a dramatic global situation humanity needs a vision of peoples living peacefully together, of ethnic and ethical groupings and of religions sharing responsibility for the care of Earth. A vision rests on hopes, goals, ideals, standards. But all over the world these have slipped from our hands. Yet we are convinced that, despite their frequent abuses and failures, it is the communities of faith who bear a responsibility to demonstrate that such hopes, ideals, and standards can be guarded, grounded, and lived. This is especially true in the modern state. Guarantees of freedom of conscience and religion are necessary but they do not substitute for binding values, convictions, and norms which are valid for all humans regardless of their social origin, sex, skin colour, language, or religion.

We are convinced of the fundamental unity of the human family on Earth. We recall the 1948 Universal Declaration of Human Rights of the United Nations. What it formally proclaimed on the level of rights we wish to confirm and deepen here from the perspective of an ethic: The full realization of the intrinsic dignity of the human person, the inalienable freedom and equality in principle of all humans, and the necessary solidarity and interdependence of all humans with each other.

On the basis of personal experiences and the burdensome history of our planet we have learned: that a better global order cannot be created or enforced by laws, prescriptions, and conventions alone; that the realization of peace, justice, and the protection of Earth depends on the insight and readiness of men and women to act justly; that action in favour of rights and freedoms presumes a consciousness of responsibility and duty, and that therefore both the minds and hearts of women and men must be addressed; that rights without morality cannot long endure, and that *there will be no better global order without a global ethic.*

By a global ethic we do not mean a global ideology or a single unified religion beyond all existing religions, and certainly not the domination of one religion over all others. By a global ethic we mean a fundamental consensus on binding values, irrevocable standards, and personal attitudes. Without such a fundamental consensus on an ethic, sooner or later every community will be threatened by chaos or dictatorship, and individuals will despair.

II. A fundamental demand: Every human being must be treated humanely

We are all fallible, imperfect men and women with limitations and defects. We know the reality of evil. Precisely because of this, we feel compelled for the sake of global welfare to express what the fundamental elements of a global ethic should be for individuals as well as for communities and organizations, for states as well as for the religions themselves. We trust that our often millennia-old religious and ethical traditions provide an ethic which is convincing and practicable for all women and men of good will, religious and non-religious.

At the same time we know that our various religious and ethical traditions often offer very different bases for what is helpful and what is unhelpful for men and women, what is right and what is wrong, what is good and what is evil. We do not wish to gloss over or ignore the serious differences among the individual religions. However, they should not hinder us from proclaiming publicly those things which we already hold in common and which we jointly affirm, each on the basis of our own religious or ethical grounds.

We know that religions cannot solve the environmental, economic, political, and social problems of Earth. However they can provide what obviously cannot be attained by economic plans, political programs, or legal regulations alone: A change in the inner orientation, the whole mentality, the "hearts" of people, and a conversion from a false path to a new orientation for life.

Humankind urgently needs social and ecological reforms, but it needs spiritual renewal just as urgently. As religious or spiritual persons we commit ourselves to this task. The spiritual powers of the religions can offer a fundamental sense of trust, a ground of meaning, ultimate standards, and a spiritual home. Of course religions are credible only when they eliminate those conflicts which spring from the religions themselves, dismantling mutual arrogance, mistrust, prejudice, and even hostile images, and thus demonstrate respect for the traditions, holy places, feasts, and rituals of people who believe differently.

Now as before, women and men are treated inhumanely all over the world. They are robbed of their opportunities and their freedom; their human rights are trampled underfoot; their dignity is disregarded. But might does not make right! In the face of all inhumanity our religious and ethical convictions demand that *every human being must be treated humanely!*

This means that every human being without distinction of age, sex, race, skin colour, physical or mental ability, language, religion, political view, or national or social origin possesses an inalienable and untouchable dignity, and everyone, the individual as well as the state, is therefore obliged to honour this dignity and protect it. Humans must always be the subjects of rights, must be ends, never mere means, never objects of commercialization and industrialization in economics, politics and media, in research institutes and industrial corporations. No one stands "above good and evil"—no human being, no social class, no influential interest group, no cartel, no police apparatus, no army, and no state. On the contrary: possessed of reason and conscience, every human is obliged to behave in a genuinely human fashion, to do good and avoid evil!

It is the intention of this Global Ethic to clarify what this means. In it we wish to recall irrevocable, unconditional ethical norms. These should not be bonds and chains, but helps and supports for people to find and realize once again their lives' direction, values, orientations, and meaning.

There is a principle which is found and has persisted in many religious and ethical traditions of humankind for thousands of years:

What you do not wish done to yourself, do not do to others, or in positive terms; *What you wish done to yourself, do to others!* This should be the irrevocable, unconditional norm for all areas of life, for families and communities, for races, nations, and religions.

Every form of egoism should be rejected: All selfishness, whether individual or collective, whether in the form of class thinking, racism, nationalism, or sexism. We condemn these because they prevent humans from being authentically human. Self-determination and self-realization are thoroughly legitimate so long as they are not separated from human self-responsibility for fellow humans and for the planet Earth.

This principle implies very concrete standards to which we humans should hold firm. From it arise four broad, ancient guidelines for human behaviour which are found in most of the religions of the world.

III. Irrevocable directives

1. Commitment to a Culture of Non-Violence and Respect for Life
Numberless women and men of all regions and religions strive to lead lives not determined by egoism but by commitment to their fellow humans and to the world around them. Nevertheless, all over the world we find endless hatred, envy, jealousy, and violence, not only between individuals but also between social and ethnic groups, between classes, races, nations, and religions. The use of violence, drug trafficking and organized crime, often equipped with new technical possibilities, has reached global proportions. Many places still are ruled by terror "from above"; dictators oppress their own people, and institutional violence is widespread. Even in some countries where laws exist to protect individual freedoms, prisoners are tortured, men and women are mutilated, hostages are killed.

a) In the great ancient religious and ethical traditions of human kind we find the directive: You shall not kill! Or in positive terms: Have respect for life! Let us reflect anew on the consequences of this ancient directive: All people have a right to life, safety, and the free development of personality insofar as they do not injure the rights of others. No one has the right physically or psychically to torture, injure, much less kill, any other human being. And no people, no state, no race, no religion has the right to hate, to discriminate against, to "cleanse," to exile, much less to liquidate a "foreign" minority which is different in behaviour or holds different beliefs.

b) Of course, wherever there are humans there will be conflicts. Such conflicts, however, should be resolved without violence within a framework of justice. This is true for states as well as for individuals. Persons who hold political power must work within the framework of a just order and commit themselves to the most non-violent, peaceful solutions possible. And they should work for this within an international order of peace which itself has need of protection and defence against perpetrators of violence. Armament is a mistaken path; disarmament is the commandment of the times. Let no one be deceived: There is no survival for humanity without global peace!

c) Young people must learn at home and in school that violence may not be a means of settling differences with others. Only thus can a culture of non-violence be created.

d) A human person is infinitely precious and must be unconditionally protected. But likewise the lives of animals and plants which inhabit this planet with us deserve protection, preservation, and care. Limitless exploitation of the natural foundations of life, ruthless destruction of the biosphere, and militarization of the cosmos are all outrages. As human beings we have a special responsibility—especially with a view to future generations—for Earth and the cosmos, for the air, water, and soil. We are all intertwined together in this cosmos and we are all dependent on each other. Each one of us depends on the welfare of all. Therefore the dominance of humanity over nature and the cosmos must not be encouraged. Instead we must cultivate living in harmony with nature and the cosmos.

e) To be authentically human in the spirit of our great religious and ethical traditions means that in public as well as in private life we must be concerned for others and ready to help. We must never be ruthless and brutal. Every people, every race, every religion must show tolerance and respect—indeed high appreciation—for every other. Minorities need protection and support, whether they be racial, ethnic, or religious.

2. Commitment to a Culture of Solidarity and a Just Economic Order

Numberless men and women of all regions and religions strive to live their lives in solidarity with one another and to work for authentic fulfilment of their vocations. Nevertheless, all over the world we find endless hunger, deficiency, and need. Not only individuals, but especially unjust institutions and structures are responsible for these tragedies. Millions of people are without work; millions are exploited by poor wages, forced to the edges of society, with their possibilities for the future destroyed. In many lands the gap between the poor and the rich, between the powerful and the powerless, is immense. We live in a world in which totalitarian state socialism as well as unbridled capitalism have hollowed out and destroyed many ethical and spiritual values. A materialistic mentality breeds greed for unlimited profit and a grasping for endless plunder. These demands claim more and more of the community's resources without obliging the individual to contribute more. The cancerous social evil of corruption thrives in the developing countries and in the developed countries alike.

a) In the great ancient religious and ethical traditions of humankind we find the directive: *You shall not steal!* Or in positive terms: *Deal honestly and fairly!* Let us reflect anew on the consequences of this ancient directive: No one has the right to rob or dispose in any way whatsoever any other person or the commonweal. Further, no one has the right to use her or his possessions without concern for the needs of society and Earth.

b) Where extreme poverty reigns, helplessness and despair spread, and theft occurs again and again for the sake of survival. Where power and wealth are accumulated ruthlessly, feelings of envy, resentment, and deadly hatred and rebellion inevitably well up in the disadvantaged and marginalized. This leads to a vicious circle of violence and counter-violence. Let no one be deceived: There is no global peace without global justice!

c) Young people must learn at home and in school that property, limited though it may be, carries with it an obligation, and that its uses should at the same time serve the common good. Only thus can a just economic order be built up.

d) If the plight of the poorest billions of humans on this planet, particularly women and children, is to be improved, the world economy must be structured more justly. Individual good deeds, and assistance projects, indispensable though they be, are insufficient. The participation of all states and the authority of international organizations are needed to build just economic institutions.

A solution which can be supported by all sides must be sought for the debt crisis and the poverty of the dissolving second world, and even more the third world. Of course conflicts of interest are unavoidable. In the developed countries, a distinction must be made between socially beneficial and non-beneficial uses of property, between justified and unjustified uses of natural resources, and between a profit-only and a socially beneficial and ecologically oriented market economy. Even the developing nations must search their national consciences.

Wherever those ruling threaten to repress those ruled, wherever institutions threaten persons, and wherever might oppresses right, we are obligated to resist—whenever possible non-violently.

e) To be authentically human in the spirit of our great religious and ethical traditions means the following:

We must utilize economic and political power for service to humanity instead of misusing it in ruthless battles for domination. We must develop a spirit of compassion with those who suffer, with a special care for the children, the aged, the poor, the disabled, the refugees, and the lonely.

We must cultivate mutual respect and consideration, so as to reach a reasonable balance of interest, instead of thinking only of unlimited power and unavoidable competitive struggles.

We must value a sense of moderation and modesty instead of an unquenchable greed for money, prestige, and consumption. In greed humans lose their "souls," their freedom, their composure, their inner peace, and thus that which makes them human.

3. Commitment to a Culture of Tolerance and a Life of Truthfulness

Numberless women and men of all regions and religions strive to lead lives of honesty and truthfulness. Nevertheless, all over the world we find endless lies and deceit, swindling and hypocrisy, ideology and demagoguery:

Politicians and business people who use lies as a means to success; Mass media which spread ideological propaganda instead of accurate reporting, misinformation instead of information, cynical commercial interest instead of loyalty to the truth; scientists and researchers who give themselves over to morally questionable ideological or political programs or to economic interest groups, or who justify research which violates fundamental ethical values; representatives of religions who dismiss other religions as of little value and who preach fanaticism and intolerance instead of respect and understanding.

a) In the great ancient religious and ethical traditions of humankind we find the directive: *You shall not lie!* Or in positive terms: *Speak and act truthfully!* Let us reflect anew on the consequences of this ancient directive: No woman or man, no institution, no state or church or religious community has the right to speak lies to other humans.

b) This is especially true for those who work in the mass media, to whom we entrust the freedom to report for the sake of truth and to whom we thus grant the office of guardian. They do not stand above morality but have the obligation to respect human dignity, human rights, and fundamental values. They are duty-bound to objectivity, fairness, and the preservation of human dignity. They have no right to intrude into individuals' private spheres, to manipulate public opinion, or to distort reality; for artists, writers, and scientists, to whom we entrust artistic and academic freedom. They are not exempt from general ethical standards and must serve the truth; for the leaders of countries, politicians, and political parties, to whom we entrust our own freedoms. When they lie in the faces of their people, when they manipulate the truth, or when they are guilty of venality or ruthlessness in domestic or foreign affairs, they forsake their credibility and deserve to lose their offices and their voters. Conversely, public opinion should support those politicians who dare to speak the truth to the people at all times; Finally, for representatives of religion. When they stir up prejudice, hatred, and enmity towards those of different belief, or even

incite or legitimate religious wars, they deserve the condemnation of human kind and the loss of their adherents. Let
no one be deceived: There is no global justice without truthfulness and humaneness!

c) Young people must learn at home and in school to think, speak,
and act truthfully. They have a right to information and
education to be able to make the decisions that will form their
lives. Without an ethical formation they will hardly be able to
distinguish the important from the unimportant. In the daily
flood of information, ethical standards will help them discern
when opinions are portrayed as facts, interests veiled, tendencies
exaggerated, and facts twisted.

d) To be authentically human in the spirit of our great religious
and ethical traditions means the following: We must not confuse
freedom with arbitrariness or pluralism with indifference to
truth. We must cultivate truthfulness in all our relationships
instead of dishonesty, dissembling, and opportunism. We must
constantly seek truth and incorruptible sincerity instead of
spreading ideological or partisan half-truths. We must coura-
geously serve the truth and we must remain constant and
trustworthy, instead of yielding to opportunistic accommodation to life.

4. Commitment to a Culture of Equal Rights and Partnership betweenMen and Women

Numberless men and women of all regions and religions strive to
live their lives in a spirit of partnership and responsible action in the
areas of love, sexuality, and family. Nevertheless, all over the world
there are condemnable forms of patriarchy, domination of one sex
over the other, exploitation of women, sexual misuse of children,
and forced prostitution. Too frequently, social inequities force
women and even children into prostitution as a means of survival—
particularly in less developed countries.

a) In the great ancient religious and ethical traditions of humankind
we find the directive: *You shall not commit sexual immorality!* Or
in positive terms: *Respect and love one another!* Let us reflect
anew on the consequences of this ancient directive: No one has

the right to degrade others to mere sex objects, to lead them into or hold them in sexual dependency.

b) We condemn sexual exploitation and sexual discrimination as one of the worst forms of human degradation. We have the duty to resist wherever the domination of one sex over the other is preached—even in the name of religious convictions; wherever sexual exploitation is tolerated, wherever prostitution is fostered or children are misused. Let no one be deceived: There is no authentic humaneness without a living together in partnership!

c) Young people must learn at home and in school that sexuality is not a negative, destructive, or exploitative force, but creative and affirmative. Sexuality is a life-affirming shaper of community which can only be effective when partners accept the responsibilities of caring for one another's happiness.

d) The relationship between women and men should be characterized not by patronizing behaviour or exploitation, but by love, partnership, and trustworthiness. Human fulfilment is not identical with sexual pleasure. Sexuality should express and reinforce a loving relationship lived by equal partners. Some religious traditions know the ideal of a voluntary renunciation of the full use of sexuality. Voluntary renunciation also can be an expression of identity and meaningful fulfilment.

e) The social institution of marriage, despite all its cultural and religious variety, is characterized by love, loyalty, and permanence. It aims at and should guarantee security and mutual support to husband, wife, and child. It should secure the rights of all family members. All lands and cultures should develop economic and social relationships which will enable marriage and family life worthy of human beings, especially for older people. Children have a right of access to education. Parents should not exploit children, nor children parents. Their relationships should reflect mutual respect, appreciation, and concern.

f) To be authentically human in the spirit of our great religious and ethical traditions means the following: We need mutual respect, partnership, and understanding, instead of patriarchal domination and degradation, which are expressions of violence and engender counter-violence. We need mutual concern, tolerance, readiness for reconciliation, and love, instead of any form of possessive lust or sexual misuse. Only what has already been experienced in personal and familial relationships can be practised on the level of nations and religions.

IV. A transformation of consciousness!

Historical experience demonstrates the following: Earth cannot be changed for the better unless we achieve a transformation in the consciousness of individuals and in public life. The possibilities for transformation have already been glimpsed in areas such as war and peace, economy, and ecology, where in recent decades fundamental changes have taken place. This transformation must also be achieved in the area of ethics and values!

Every individual has intrinsic dignity and inalienable rights, and each also has an inescapable responsibility for what she or he does and does not do. All our decisions and deeds, even our omissions and failures, have consequences.

Keeping this sense of responsibility alive, deepening it and passing it on to future generations, is the special task of religions.

We are realistic about what we have achieved in this consensus, and so we urge that the following be observed:

1. A universal consensus on many disputed ethical questions (from bio- and sexual ethics through mass media and scientific ethics to economic and political ethics) will be difficult to attain. Nevertheless, even for many controversial questions, suitable solutions should be attainable in the spirit of the fundamental principles we have jointly developed here.
2. In many areas of life a new consciousness of ethical responsibility has already arisen. Therefore we would be pleased if as many professions as possible, such as those of physicians, scientists, business people, journalists, and politicians, would develop up-to-date codes of ethics which would provide specific guidelines for the vexing questions of these particular professions.
3. Above all, we urge the various communities of faith to formulate their very specific ethics: What does each faith tradition have to say, for example, about the meaning of life and death, the enduring of suffering and the forgiveness of guilt, about selfless sacrifice and

the necessity of renunciation, about compassion and joy. These will deepen, and make more specific, the already discernible global ethic.

In conclusion, we appeal to all the inhabitants of this planet. Earth cannot be changed for the better unless the consciousness of individuals is changed. We pledge to work for such transformation in individual and collective consciousness, for the awakening of our spiritual powers through reflection, meditation, prayer, or positive thinking, for a conversion of the heart. Together we can move mountains! Without a willingness to take risks and a readiness to sacrifice there can be no fundamental change in our situation! Therefore we commit ourselves to a common global ethic, to better mutual understanding, as well as to socially beneficial, peace-fostering, and Earth-friendly ways of life.

Guidelines for Inter-Faith Dialogue of the Anglican Church of Canada

*T*hese guidelines are offered to Canadian Anglicans as they seek to reach out to their neighbours of other faiths. Our approach has two separate, but inter-related aspects: *dialogue*, which includes growing in our knowledge of each other and a mutual sharing of spiritual insights; and *common action* which would involve joint efforts to deal with issues related to life together in society, but might also include activities of a devotional nature.

A   The Path of Dialogue

1. Meet the people themselves and get to know their traditions.

In many Canadian communities there are places of worship of the world's great religions. Several of these religious communities have national or regional organizations, and frequently people with responsibility for inter-faith dialogue and cooperation. There are also bodies that have as their purpose the fostering of better relationships among people of different faith communities.

2. Wherever possible, engage in dialogue ecumenically.

When we seek to explain ourselves to others the differences between Christians take on a different perspective. An ecumenical approach to dialogue allows us to focus on those things which are essential in Christian teaching. While individual approaches need not be discouraged, a ministerial or local council of churches might well be the appropriate body to initiate dialogue. Generally, dialogue is best done by representatives of several churches at the same time.

3. Allow others to speak for themselves.

Too often stereotypes have kept us apart from people of other faiths. One obvious way of avoiding this is to let the dialogue partners describe themselves, as we expect to speak for ourselves. This is not to say that our listening must always be uncritical. Our questions will only be accepted as we show that we want to learn and understand. One way to ensure this kind of balance is to involve dialogue partners in the planning process itself.

4. Be aware of other loyalties.

We always bring into relationships a cluster of theological commitments and cultural loyalties. An awareness of this can avoid unrealistic expectations, and can help focus on central rather than peripheral issues. Acknowledgement of our own and others' loyalties can pave the way to deeper sharing.

5. Prepare carefully for the dialogue.

No dialogue venture will be successful without sensitive planning and preparation.

    a) It is important to approach others with the same kind of respect we would wish to be accorded. They cherish their beliefs and practices as deeply as we do our own, however different they may appear to us.

b) Every religious tradition, including our own, has unworthy adherents and unpleasant episodes in its history. True dialogue is not possible if only the best of one tradition is contrasted with the worst of others.

c) Issues of separation must be addressed as well as those of unity. Dialogue is not furthered when painful or difficult areas are glossed over. However, this should not be done with an attitude of superiority or solely in an effort to air grievances. It should include an awareness of our own contribution to division and misunderstanding.

d) By engaging in dialogue Christians are not being asked to compromise their faith that God was revealed in the person of Christ. Their understanding of their own faith should be clear, so that the Christian perspective can be fairly presented to dialogue partners. Dialogue, however, should not be a subtle form of proselytizing, but an occasion for mutual sharing.

B   The Path of Common Action

1. Deal with issues related to living together as part of the human community.

This may well be the basis upon which dialogue begins. Our planet is too small and the problems confronting it too great for people of faith to attempt to work in isolation or from a position of conflict. Some matters on which inter-faith cooperation is possible include:

a) Joint approaches to government on matters of economic, social, political and cultural concern.

b) Urging respect for human rights and religious freedom not only for ourselves but for others also.

c) Coordinated efforts to deal with global issues such as world peace, the environment or hunger.

2. Foster efforts at education and communication between people of different faiths.

Education is both a consequence of and a way into inter-faith dialogue. The effort to learn and understand will bring us into closer contact, while that contact will lead us to want to share our learning with others.

a) In our pluralist society it is important that people have an appreciation of the rich religious heritage of those who make up our community. People are pleased, for example, when their major religious festivals are acknowledged. These can provide the occasion for learning more about the faith concerned.

b) Sustained contact with people of other faiths can begin to break down false images with which many of us have grown up, and to which we are still often exposed. Efforts should be made to challenge such stereotypes wherever they may be encountered, including those in our own educational and liturgical material.

c) Among the places on which such educational efforts can be focused are: schools, universities, and other institutions for adult education, seminaries and church schools.

d) Inaccurate media coverage of minority religious groups can be detrimental. Positive relations should be developed with the media so that their potential for increasing public awareness about people of different faiths can be fully utilized.

e) Efforts should also be made to sensitize travellers to the religious traditions of the countries they visit, and to encourage them to share their experiences on their return.

f) Representatives of other faith groups should be consulted, and where possible involved, in the preparation of educational material that touches on their history, beliefs and practices.

3. Share spiritual insights and approaches.

There is much that religious people can share of their spiritual insights in an atmosphere of learning and openness. However, people of other traditions are no more anxious than we are to engage in acts of worship which blur very real differences of theology or world-view. Neither do they relish the appropriation by others of their religious symbols or sacred texts. However, there is much that religious people can share of their spiritual insights in an atmosphere of learning and openness.

a) Attendance at another community's acts of worship should always be accompanied by careful preparation and an opportunity to ask questions afterward, preferably answered by members of that tradition.

b) Christians who are present during the worship of another faith community may be unable to participate fully in everything that is said and done, but they should attend with the attitude that the event is an important part of the spiritual life of the participants.

c) Prayer for people of other religious traditions is valuable, especially during times of particular need or when it is for better relationships with them. Some Christians feel that they should pray for the conversion of others to Christ, while others would argue that this should not be done. In any event it is God who converts people. Christians themselves are far from fully understanding or obeying God's will. It is inappropriate to single out any one religious group as being in particular need of conversion in a way that fosters prejudice against them.

Because the encounter with each group is distinctive there can be no one set of guidelines which will cover all situations. Until our encounters reach the point of allowing each party to express freely its sense of spiritual reality, the meeting is more likely to be curious than serious. The simplest instruction may well be that of St. Augustine, based on Jesus' twofold commandment, which is to love God and do what you will. Love, in the sense of mutuality, means that as we would share what is most precious to us, the gift in Christ Jesus, so we must invite others to share their treasures with us.

Select
Bibliography

There is a large and growing body of literature that focuses on world religions and the various Christian responses to them. Some of it can be classified as "comparative studies" describing the general doctrines, beliefs, worship, and practices of the major religions. Much of it has to do with specific bi-lateral and multi-lateral dialogues, such as Christian-Buddhist and Christian-Jewish-Muslim dialogues, as well as extensive commentary on anti-Semitism and the Jewish Holocaust in Europe.

There are specialist discussions of particular ethical or social concerns, such as the environment, peace, disarmament, poverty, the role of women, and homosexuality, and their treatment by the world's religions. The list is far too long to be helpful in a book like this.

What follows therefore is a small and select bibliography of books for the interested general reader who is perhaps new to this area and wishes to read more. Most of these were written within the last fifteen years and some contain further bibliographies that will guide the reader onwards.

The Asian Journal of Thomas Merton. Toronto: McClelland & Stewart, 1973.

The Bible and People of Other Faiths. Wesley Ariarajah. Geneva: World Council of Churches Risk Publications, 1985.

Christianity and Other Religions. John Hick and Brian Hebblethwaite, eds. San Francisco: Collins, 1980.

Christians and Religious Pluralism: Patterns in the Christian Theology of Religions. Allan Race. Philadelphia: SCM Press, 1983.

Christianity and the World Religions: Paths of Dialogue with Islam, Hinduism and Buddhism. Hans Küng. New York: Doubleday, 1988.

Christian Uniqueness Reconsidered: The Myth of A Pluralistic Theology of Religions. Gavin d'Costa, ed. Maryknoll: Orbis Books, 1990.

Christianity Without Absolutes. Reinhold Bernhardt. Philadelphia: SCM Press, 1994.

The Dialogical Imperative. David Lochhead. Maryknoll: Orbis Books, 1988.

The Eliade Guide to World Religions. Mircea Eliade and I.P. Couliano, eds. New York: Harper, 1991.

Global Responsibility: In Search of A New World Ethic. Hans Küng. New York: Crossroad, 1991.

Global 2000 Revisited. Gerald O. Barney, ed. Chicago: The Millennium Institute, 1993.

God and the Universe of Faiths. John Hick. San Francisco: Collins, 1973.

The Gospel in A Pluralist Society. Lesslie Newbigin. London: SPCK, 1989.

A History of God: The 4000 Year Quest of Judaism, Christianity and Islam. Karen Armstrong. New York: Ballantine, 1993.

Love Meets Wisdom: A Christian Experience of Buddhism. Aloysius Pieris. Maryknoll: Orbis Books, 1988.

The Marriage of East and West. Bede Griffiths. Springfield: Collins, 1982.

Meditations with Mechtild of Magdeburg. Sue Woodruff. Sante Fe: Bear & Company, 1982.

Meditations with Meister Eckhart. Matthew Fox. Sante Fe: Bear & Company, 1982.T

The Myth of Christian Uniqueness. John Hick and Paul F. Knitter, eds. Maryknoll: Orbis Books, 1987.

No Other Name? A Critical Story of Christian Attitudes Toward the World Religions. Paul F. Knitter. Philadelphia: SCM Press, 1985.

One Earth: Many Religions. Paul F. Knitter. Maryknoll: Orbis Books, 1995.

Pilgrimage of Hope. Marcus Braybrooke. New York: Crossroad, 1992.

Pluralism: Challenge to World Religions. Harold Coward. Maryknoll: Orbis Books, 1985.

Source Book for the Community of Religions. Joel D. Beversluis, ed. Chicago: Council for the Parliament of the World's Religions, 1993.

Theology and Religious Pluralism. Gavin d'Costa. Oxford: Blackwell, 1986.

To Meet and To Greet. Kenneth Cragg. Philadelphia: Epworth Press, 1992.

Toward A Renewed Understanding of Ecumenism. The United Church of Canada. Toronto: 1994.

Toward A Theology for Inter-Faith Dialogue. Anglican Consultative Council. London: 1984.

Toward A World Theology. Wilfred Cantwell-Smith. New York: MacMillan, 1981.

Towards A New Relationship: Christians and People of Other Faiths. Kenneth Cracknell. Philadelphia: Epworth Press, 1986.

The Transcendent Unity of Religions. Frithjof Schuon. Wheaton: The Theosophical Publishing House, 1993.

World Scripture: A Comparative Anthology of Sacred Texts. Andrew Wilson, ed. New York: Paragon House, 1995.

The Unknown Christ of Hinduism. Raimundo Panikkar. London: Longman & Todd, 1968.